The Jews in Late Antiquity

PAST IMPERFECT

Overviews of the latest research by the world's leading scholars. Subjects cross the full range of fields in the period ca. 400—1500 CE which, in a European context, is known as the Middle Ages. Anyone interested in this period will be enthralled and enlightened by these overviews, written in provocative but accessible language. These affordable paperbacks prove that the era still retains a powerful resonance and impact throughout the world today.

Director and Editor-in-Chief

Simon Forde, 's-Hertogenbosch

Acquisitions Editors

Erin T. Dailey, *Leeds*
Ruth Kennedy, *Adelaide*

Production

Ruth Kennedy, *Adelaide*

Cover Design

Martine Maguire-Weltecke, *Dublin*

The Jews in Late Antiquity

Rodrigo Laham Cohen

British Library Cataloguing in Publication Data
A catalogue record for this book is available from the British Library.

© **2018, Arc Humanities Press, Leeds**

ISBN (print): 9781942401650
eISBN (PDF): 9781942401667
eISBN (EPUB): 9781942401674

arc-humanities.org
Printed and bound by CPI Group (UK) Ltd, Croydon, CR0 4YY

Contents

Introduction

Surely it is time to break with the lachrymose theory of pre-Revolutionary woe, and to adopt a view more in accord with historic truth (Baron 1928, 526).

More than eighty years have passed since Salo Baron's "Ghetto and Emancipation", whose words had such a major impact on Jewish historiography. Gradually, Jewish and non-Jewish scholars began to highlight not only a history of segregation, persecution, and massacres, but also interaction and coexistence. However, some researchers inverted the terms and built a rosy picture of Jewish life during late antiquity and the early Middle Ages. Thus, Jewish communities from Italy, Gaul, the Balkans, North Africa, Palestine, Babylonia, and even Spain were seen as untroubled groups in the period. Seizures of synagogues, expulsions, and forced conversions were analyzed as exceptions. It was suggested that only after the First Crusade in 1096 CE did the situation of Jewish people change in Europe. In the same vein, it was affirmed that Jewish settlements in the Land of Israel and Babylonia suffered no major religious problems.

However, each Jewish community must be analyzed in its specific context. This may seem like an obvious statement to make, but it is important to keep that in mind. There are several Jewish histories in late antiquity, not just one. Even if we accepted that there was a common Judaism, we have to consider that the Jews of Visigothic Toledo, Papal Rome, and Babylonian Pumbedita were surrounded by different societies and realities. We can discuss the level of isolation each Jewish group experienced, but to sustain the idea of a complete separation is to ignore the sources.

In this sense we present the history of the Jews in late antiquity by focussing on regions. We do not neglect the possibility of making generalizations. In fact, common patterns will be identified. But it is very important to be clear about regional and temporal differences between each distinct case study.

When Baron wrote the article quoted above, late antiquity had not yet been recognized as a specific historical period. As every historiographical (and artificial) construct, it is not easy to explain in few words the key features of the period. However, we can say that the idea of *Spätantike*[1] was coined to illuminate continuities after the debated "fall" of the Western Roman Empire in 476 CE. Of course, there are still ongoing controversies around the period's characteristics and its precise time frame but this is not the place to examine those topics. Suffice to say, it is important to clarify that this study is mainly focussed on the period between the third and seventh centuries CE.[2]

The book is organized into eight chapters. The first presents the problem of sources and other methodological issues. Then, we analyze different regions: Italy, North Africa (except Egypt), Gaul, Spain, Egypt, the Land of Israel, and Babylonia. Due to space constraints, very important Jewish settlements in the Balkans—including Greece—Asia Minor, and Syria will not be considered.

Due to the characteristics of this short book, only a brief study of each case has been presented. Thus, investigations and historiographical controversies are condensed. For that reason, we strongly recommend reading the cited bibliography for a better comprehension of each region. *The Jews in Late Antiquity* should be considered as a first step toward the understanding of a little-known period in Jewish history.

Notes

[1] Although Peter Brown popularized the category in his seminal book *The World of Late Antiquity* (1971), Alois Riegl was the first historian that used the expression—in German—in 1901.

[2] The most common criterion for late antiquity is to take the Crisis of the Third Century (ca. 235–284) in the Roman Empire as a starting point and the rise of Islam as the final event (ca. seventh century).

Chapter 1

The Problem of Sources

The reconstruction of Jewish life in the past should comprise the analysis of written and archaeological sources. Certainly, Jewish texts are essential to understanding intracommunal dynamics. However, Jewish voices have not always survived. As we will see, this is the case with Jewish communities in Europe and Africa during late antiquity. In contrast, there was a prolific production of Jewish writings in Palestine and Babylonia. Rabbinical Judaism—a new Judaism—created the *Mishnah*, the *Tosefta*, the *Jerusalem Talmud* (*Yerushalmi*), and the *Babylonian Talmud* (*Bavli*), among other texts. Nevertheless, rabbinical writings are not only difficult to analyze but also problematic to date as they include oral traditions. In addition, the *Talmud*'s ahistorical, performative, and legal nature complicates our understanding of Jewish history.

We can improve our knowledge of Jews by turning to a different type of evidence. First of all, there are texts referring to Jews written by other groups. Pagan[1] and Christian texts—used carefully—can illuminate interaction among communities in the period, and even aspects of Jewish customs. Second, Jewish epigraphy—mainly epitaphs—offers brief but first-hand information about Jewish geography, languages, ideas, and traditions, among other features. Finally, Jewish archaeological remains—chiefly synagogues and cemeteries—help us to hypothesize about architectural patterns, liturgy, communal life, and other religious and non-religious aspects. Other artifacts, such as seals, bowls, or talismans are also useful.

Silences in the West

Flavius Josephus died ca. 100 CE.[2] There is a hiatus of almost 800 years after his death until we find another text written by Jews in Europe. *Sefer Josippon* is difficult to date, but it was written in southern Italy, probably between the ninth and tenth centuries.[3] Additionally, Shabbethai Donnolo wrote on medicine, astrology, and religion—also in southern Italy—in the mid-tenth century.[4] While Josephus—born in the Land of Israel—wrote in Greek, Donnolo—born in Italy—wrote in Hebrew. Jews were different: late antiquity had changed them.

There are only three European late ancient texts, the Jewish authorship and dating of which are controversial: the *Collatio legum Mosaicarum et Romanarum*, the *Epistola Anne ad Senecam*, and the *Liber Antiquitatum Biblicarum*. All are anonymous and they have no clear dating or geographical references. The *Collatio* is a comparison of Jewish and Roman Law. It is usually dated to the fourth century but there are debates around its Jewish or Christian origin.[5] The *Epistola* is a treatise against idolatry and considered to have been written between the fourth and fifth century. The religion of its author has also been debated.[6] The *Liber*—also known as *Pseudo-Philo* due to its similarity to Philo's texts—is harder to date because it is a late Latin translation from a Greek text, originally written in Hebrew around the first century CE.[7] Even if we accept the Jewish authorship of these three texts, they do not give us valuable information about Jewish life. Did late ancient European

Jews write historical texts that are now lost? As Yosef Hayim Yerushalmi (1982) has shown, there is not a simple answer to this question. Be it as it may, the only Jewish European texts written in late antiquity that have survived are epitaphs and synagogal inscriptions.

Rabbinic Literature as a Problem

The times in which rabbinic literature was not considered a historical source are long gone. Nowadays, most researchers employ both the *Talmudim* and other rabbinical texts in order to reconstruct Jewish history in the Land of Israel and Mesopotamia.

Nevertheless, there are still problems. The first is dating. Both *Talmudim* (the *Yerushalmi* and the *Bavli*) are composed of the *Mishnah* and a commentary, the *Gemara.* Most scholars (Strack and Stemberger 1996) consider that the *Mishnah* was written in the first part of the third century CE. It is accepted, also, that the *Yerushalmi* was edited between the fourth and fifth centuries CE and the *Bavli* between the sixth and seventh CE (Strack and Stemberger 1996; Halivni 2013). However, both *corpora* are presented as compilations of laws, opinions, and tales formulated by different rabbinical generations, beginning in the second century BCE. Thus, there are sentences attributed to five pairs of sages called *zugot* (second BCE–first CE), others to the *tannaim* (first CE–third CE) and the majority to the *amoraim* (third CE–sixth CE).[8] However, the role of the final editors of the *Talmundin* is strongly debated. Did they alter previous traditions? Did they create opinions and attribute them to older generations? Indeed, certain scholars have argued that there was a special group of rabbis that worked after the *amoraim* and influenced the final edition of the *Bavli*: the *stammaim* (Halivni 2013). We will return to this topic in Chapter 8.

A second problem is the absence of other texts connected directly with rabbinic literature. In that light, there are relatively few opportunities to contrast rabbinical affirmations with other non-rabbinical (Jewish or non-Jewish) sources.[9] Consequently, we depend strongly on internal evidence to corroborate talmudic information.

Finally, the *Talmudim* were not written as historical texts. They contain striking inconsistences and anachronisms. It is not easy to confirm whether rabbis lacked historic knowledge or if they decided to avoid the historical genre. In this sense, Yerushalmi (1982, 10) considered, "Israel is told only that it must be a kingdom of priests and a holy people; nowhere is it suggested that it become a nation of historians."

Fortunately, there are alternatives that help us to flesh out the picture. Let's take a look at them next.

Filling in the Gap

As indicated earlier, it is crucial to analyze non-Jewish evidence in order to reconstruct the history of Jewish settlements. For late antiquity, there is a strong dependence on Christian texts, but sometimes pagan texts also help. Certainly, each kind of Christian or pagan source provides us with different information. We find more information about *historical Jews* in chronicles and letters, and we are presented mainly with *hermeneutical Jews* in theological tractates.[10]

In fact, the so-called Christian *adversus Iudaeos* (against the Jews) literature was ubiquitous in late antiquity (Fredriksen and Irshai 2006). The vast majority of the Fathers of the Church frequently attacked Jews in their writings. Accusations such as spiritual blindness, perfidy, wickedness, hardheartedness, and deicide, among others, were continuously repeated. Jews were said to have abandoned God and been abandoned by Him: Gentiles replaced Jews in the divine plan.

Why did the Church Fathers write against Jews during late antiquity? It is a significant historiographical debate. On the one hand, it was stated that *adversus Iudaeos* literature was the result of a real conflict between Jews and Christians, mainly between orthodoxies. Thus, in a context where the Jewish religion was still passively or actively attracting Christians, bishops, discursively, and sometimes physically, attacked Jews in order to restrict the interaction. This was the main thesis of Marcel Simon (1948), who stated that at the heart of anti-Judaism lay the pro-Judaism of the common people. On the other hand, Rosemary Ruether (1974), reformulating previous analysis,[11] suggested that anti-Judaism was inextricably linked to Christian theology. According to Ruether, the Fathers of the Church had to use anti-Jewish tropes to explain God's plan. In accordance with this position, there can be anti-Judaism without *historical Jews*.

These perspectives are not mutually exclusive. Each anti-Jewish text has to be analyzed to understand whether it was written due to a real problem among the actual communities or not. This is very important because we are trying to find not only *rhetorical* or *hermeneutical Jews*, but also *historical Jews*. Even though it is important to be acquainted with the image of the Jews in Christian texts, we have to be able to discriminate between clichés and useful data. Although non-Jewish texts are fundamental in regions where no texts written by Jews survived, they are also important in Palestine and Babylonia. Not only do they offer images of the Jews, they also provide information to compare with rabbinical sources.

However, the risk of using non-Jewish sources must be emphasized. They, self-evidently, offer an external and partial point of view, mostly with polemical aims.

Furthermore, Christians sometimes used the term "Jew" to attack other Christians—seen as heretics—who had no relation to Jews. In addition, Christian texts usually do not show any internal aspects of Jewish communities.

Epigraphy—text written on hard material—is also a useful tool. Currently, there is no serious historian who rejects the possibilities that inscriptions offer to any research. Of course, epigraphy should not be overestimated, but it does provide some clues about settlements, languages, names, economic activities, communal offices, etc. Unfortunately, most Jewish inscriptions in late antiquity are concise. There are also serious problems with identifying and dating the material (Van der Horst 2014).

The geographical distribution of the epigraphic evidence does not always have an explanation. For example, there are more than 600 recorded inscriptions in the Jewish catacombs of Rome, but no more than twenty in Alexandria (Van der Horst 2014, 21). The Jewish community of Rome was large, but according to written sources the Alexandrian one was bigger. In this sense, the absence of epigraphy does not mean an absence of Jews. Furthermore, identifying an inscription as Jewish is not as straightforward as it may sound (Van der Horst 2014, 9–12). Not every inscription includes a Semitic name, words in Hebrew, a *menorah* (seven-armed candelabrum),[12] or Judaic religious references. In fact, Jews tended to use non-Jewish names and the language of the region. Sometimes an inscription is recognized as Jewish merely because it was found at a Jewish burial place. But if an isolated inscription is uncovered and there are no clear identity markers, it is impossible to determine the Jewishness of the person buried.

In addition, only in a few regions are there inscriptions that cover long periods of time. The Jewish-Italian epigraphic record is a good example. In fact, inscriptions from Rome are dated between the second and fifth centuries CE. After that no Jewish late ancient inscription is found in the city. But we know—thanks to Christian sources—that Jews remained in the city. Thus, if we want to conduct extensive research, it is necessary to analyze inscriptions from other Italian cities such as Venosa or Taranto, where there are inscriptions dated between the fifth and ninth centuries CE. It is then possible to compare and hypothesize the evolution of Italian Jewish communities. However, it is not clear whether there was a long-term change or if each region had its own development.

The situation in the Land of Israel is different. The epigraphic record is more complete and allows internal changes to be tracked. In contrast, there are no Jewish inscriptions in Mesopotamia, except for texts written on seals and incantation bowls. The extensive rabbinical written production is not complemented by a rich epigraphic record.

Regarding archaeology, identifying archaeological remains as Jewish can be challenging. Obviously, an inscription *in situ* helps to recognize a building as Jewish. Art also facilitates the identification of synagogues, houses, or cemeteries. Sometimes depictions of a *menorah,* an *etrog* (a yellow citron fruit used during the festival of *Sukkot*), a *lulav* (a closed frond of the date palm tree, also used in *Sukkot*), a *shofar* (a ritual musical instrument made from ram's horn or another animal sanctioned for the purpose), or a Torah Ark, are found on walls or pavements. Certain architectural features—an *aedicula* to place the Torah— also give hints that help to identify the Jewish character of the place.

However, Jews shared architectural and artistic features with non-Jewish groups. Even though there were specific Jewish icons such as the *menorah*, synagogues also employed iconography that is generally considered to be pagan. Thus, zodiacs—even images of Helios—were found in Palestinian synagogues and certain pagan figures were discovered in the Jewish Roman catacombs. Indeed, artistic motifs like animals and flowers were similar in pagan, Christian, and Jewish buildings. In fact, there is a consensus that all religious groups used the same workshops (Rutgers 1995, 67–99), and there is an ongoing debate around the concept of *Jewish art* in late antiquity (Elsner 2003).

In the same vein, there was not a unique building shape for synagogues: frequently synagogues were architecturally similar to other buildings in the same city. The *Bavli*, in *b* (=*Bavli, Babylonian Talmud*) *Shabbat* 72b, seems to appreciate this similarity when considering the situation of a Jew who thought he was in front of a synagogue but was actually at a pagan temple.

Archaeological remains of synagogues are few and far between in the Diaspora (Hachlili 1998; Levine 2005), but plentiful in Palestine. In fact, only two ancient synagogues have been found in Western Europe (see Chapter 2), one in North Africa (see Chapter 3), five in the Balkans[13], two in Asia Minor[14], and two in Syria[15], while more than sixty have been excavated in the Land of Israel, mainly in Galilee (Milson 2007, 301–476; Hachlili 2013, 683–84). As we will see, catacombs, cemeteries, and houses have also been unearthed.

Notes

[1] Although "pagan" is a biased and inaccurate concept, we will use it to refer to non-Jews, who are also neither Christians nor Muslims.

[2] Josephus was born in Palestine but he moved to Rome after the fall of Jerusalem in 70 CE. On Josephus and his historical work, see Rodgers 2007.

[3] On the dating and significance of *Jossipon*, see Dönitz 2012.

[4] On Donnolo, see Mancuso 2010, 1–76.

[5] On the *Collatio*, see Frakes 2011, who affirms that the text was written by a Christian.

[6] Ramelli (2004) states that the document was produced by a Christian author.

[7] See Murphy 1993. The only aspect of this historic document that can provide information about Jews is the fact that it was translated into Latin during late antiquity. However, a new insight on the *Liber Antiquitatum Biblicarum* can be found in Heil 2017, where the author suggests the possibility that the text had been originally written in Latin in the context of a non-rabbinic Western European Jewish culture.

[8] For a still valuable and complete introduction to the *Talmudim,* see Strack and Stemberger 1996.

[9] Certainly, rabbinic literature was not uniform. As Philip Alexander (2010, 9–11) has stated, not all texts that are described as *rabbinical* can be easily aligned with core rabbinical texts (*Mishnah, Talmudim,* and early *midrashim*). Thus, certain *midrashim, targumim,* and *piyyutim* are usually seen as rabbinical but are considerably different from *Talmudim.* The same position can be held with *hekhalot* literature and, more clearly, *Sefer Zerubbabel* and *Pirke de-Rabbi Eliezer.* Notwithstanding, this is not the place to discuss the boundaries of rabbinic literature.

[10] Jeremy Cohen (1999, 2–3) saw the *Hermeneutical Jew* as "constructed in the discourse of Christian theology, and above all in Christian theologians' interpretation of Scripture." Fredriksen (2013, 249) used the term "Hermeneutical Jew" ("The 'Jew' as a Figure for Wrongly Reading the Bible"), as opposed to "Rhetorical Jew" ("The 'Jew' as a Polemic Anti-Self") and "Real Jew."

[11] In the latter part of nineteenth century, Adolf von Harnack considered Jews to be straw men in Christian texts.

[12] On the *menorah* and its significance, see Hachlili 2001.

[13] Saranda (fifth–sixth centuries); Stobi (second–fourth centuries); Philippopolis (third–fifth centuries), now Plovdiv in Bulgaria; Aegina (fourth century). The Delos synagogue is the earliest in the Diaspora (second century BCE), although its identification as a synagogue is not undisputed.

[14] Sardis (third–sixth centuries) and Priene (second–third centuries). There are doubts about possible synagogal remains in Miletus, Pergamum, Mopsuestia, and, most recently, Limyra.

[15] Apamea (fourth–fifth centuries) and Dura Europos (second–third centuries).

Chapter 2

Italy

As we can read in Josephus and Philo, the Jewish community in Rome was prominent between the first century BCE
and first CE (Cappelletti 2006; Simonsohn 2014). Roman
Jews, however, were not of central concern for pagan
writers, who mentioned Jews only marginally.[1] Although
many Jews arrived in Rome after the destruction of the
Second Temple in 70 CE—the Arch of Titus is a permanent
testimony of that fact—the life of Italian Jews continued
without major changes.

   Six Jewish catacombs—dated between the second and
fifth centuries—were found in the city. Even though three
were destroyed in modern times due to landslides, previous explorers took notes of inscriptions and there are
now more than six hundred Jewish epitaphs registered.[2]
Thanks to epigraphy, we know that there were at least
twelve synagogues in the city, although we do not know if
they were active at the same time. We also know that Greek
was the predominant language. This does not mean that
Jews spoke Greek: the epigraphic language does not always
coincide with the spoken one. In this sense, it is important
to keep in mind that Greek was also a sacred language
for the Jews in antiquity. In contrast, it is surprising that
Hebrew—and Aramaic—represents less than 2 per cent
of the record. It is likely that the Jewish communities of

Rome opted for Greek as a sacred language and Latin as a quotidian one. Finally, no rabbi is mentioned in Roman inscriptions: *Archisynagogos, gerusiarch, archon, grammateus, Father of the synagogue, Mother of the synagogue,* are all acknowledged but no rabbi.[3] This probably means that the rabbinization process generated in the Land of Israel did not reach Italy (and Europe) until the sixth century at the earliest (Schwartz 2002). Only in that century—in Venosa—is a rabbi mentioned in a Jewish inscription.[4] The rabbinization of Italy can also be observed when comparing Roman inscriptions with those from southern Italy (mainly from Venosa). In ninth-century Venosa, Jews not only date their epitaphs according to the falling of the Second Temple, but also use Hebrew as the primary epigraphic language.[5] Talmudic fragments and *piyyutim*[6] from Palestine are also found in ninth-century epitaphs from Venosa. In terms of onomastics, a similar change can be detected: from less than 20 per cent in late ancient Rome, Semitic names became preponderant in early medieval Venosa.[7]

Concerning occupations, only four mentions of economic activities are found in Roman inscriptions.[8] In contrast, several Jews decided to record religious offices on their relatives' graves. Religion was more important than economic activity, at least at the time of death. Regarding iconography, typical Jewish symbols of the late ancient period are found in the catacombs: *menorah, etrog, shofar, lulav,* Torah shrine, etc. These symbols were found not only on the tombstones, but also on *lucernae* (lamps), sarcophagi, and gold glasses (Rutgers 1995). Furthermore, as we will see in other regions, neutral (flowers, animals, etc.) and even pagan imagery was also found in catacombs. There are controversies around the Jewish use—or not—of the pagan representations found in the catacomb of *Vigna Randanini* (Cappelletti 2006, 155–56). Beyond that, human reliefs and other pagan imagery were also found on Jewish sarcophagi.

Even though inscriptions referred to synagogues in Rome, no archaeological remains were uncovered. However, ancient synagogues were discovered in Ostia and Bova Marina. The Ostia synagogue was found in 1961. Its identification was simple thanks to inscriptions and Jewish iconography *in situ*. The building was built ca. first century CE and was reformed in the fourth.[9] The existence of a synagogue of a considerable size revealed the importance of the local Jewish community. In addition, it was not only a preaching space but also a complex that included numerous rooms (the specific uses of which are yet to be identified), a kitchen, and probably a *Mikvah* (a bath used for ritual immersion) outside. Furthermore, the place for the Torah was modernized in the fourth century, implying the growth of the Torah's role in the liturgy. The synagogue was abandoned—no sign of destruction or reutilization was found—between the fourth and fifth centuries, probably due to the decline of the city.[10]

The Bova Marina synagogue was uncovered in the 1980s. Although the finding was not as famed as the Ostia synagogue, it was significant for many reasons. On the one hand, except for an indirect reference in the *Codex Theodosianus* and an inscription from Reggio di Calabria (fifty kilometres from Bova Marina) there had been no evidence of a Jewish community in the area. On the other hand, the synagogue was probably built in the fourth century CE, reformed in the sixth and destroyed in some point between that century and the seventh. Those dates are important because, according to Theodosian and Justinian codes, since the fifth century no synagogue was permitted to be reformed or ornamented.[11] Thus, these archaeological remains help us to call into question the application of the Roman legislation. The synagogue was easily identified because of a mosaic pavement with

Jewish iconography: *menorah*, *etrog*, and *shofar*. There is a debate around the building's location. Certain authors considered it to be a rural synagogue, while others suggested that the site was not well excavated and, because of that, only a few structures were detected (Costamagna 2003). However, Bova Marina was not particularly large and, as we will see in Gregory the Great's *Registrum*, there were Jewish peasants in late ancient Italy (by the end of the sixth century).

The Bova Marina synagogue was destroyed: signs of fire and abandoned coins were found in the ruins. The destruction could be seen as the result not of anti-Jewish aggression but of a Lombard attack that devastated not only Jewish buildings but also the entire region.[12]

Returning to legislation, it is important to remark that after Constantine, and—even more so—Theodosius, the situation of the Jewish communities in the Roman Empire changed. It was not an immediate transformation, but Jews were gradually marginalized. In fact, the *Codex Theodosianus*—a compilation of Roman Laws published by Theodosius II in 438—shows the juridical subordination of the Jews, who were allowed to remain and practice their religion but under Christian control and regulation (Linder 1987; Nemo-Pekelman 2010). Thus, among other laws, conversion to Judaism was punished: Jews were expelled from public administration and the army, they were not allowed to have Christian slaves, and, as mentioned above, new synagogues were not permitted to be built nor old ones to be renovated. In contrast, old synagogues were protected against attacks, the *Sabbath* was respected, and violence against Jews discouraged. It is worth mentioning that it is difficult to determine the degree of application of the law. In addition, the Theodosian Code was promulgated throughout the whole empire, though it was used more in the west.

The language employed in the *Codex* was very aggressive because it incorporated language from the Church. Even in the laws that protect Judaism, Jews were called *nefaria secta* or *superstitio*, among other negative epithets. As stated previously, during late antiquity the Fathers of the Church attacked Jews discursively time and again. Indeed, it is impossible to summarize all the vilifications of Judaism written by Italian bishops during the fourth and fifth centuries. Ambrose of Milan (ca. 340–397), Gautentius of Brescia (*d.* 410), Chromatius of Aquileia (*d.* ca. 407), and Maximus of Turin (ca. 380–ca. 423) are only some examples of clerics who wrote against Jews. Nevertheless, as stated before, most of the references to Jews in sermons, homilies, treatises, and even letters do not provide information about *historical Jews.* Even if those churchmen wrote in relation to an existing problem with Jews, they did not provide much information about Jewish life. Words related to hardheartedness, carnality, deicide, or simply general references to biblical Jews, constitute the bulk of the material related to Judaism.

Nonetheless, sometimes it is possible to extract some information. Ambrose, for example, had a dispute with Emperor Theodosius following the destruction of a synagogue in *Callinicum* (now Al-Raqqah, in Syria) in 388. The emperor wanted a local bishop to pay for the reconstruction of the Jewish building but Ambrose opposed. During the communications (only Ambrose's letters survived), the bishop of Milan mentioned the burning of a synagogue in Italy, probably in Milan.[13]

One century later, Pope Gelasius I (*d.* 496), sent two letters related to Jews. In the first, he referred to a Jew called *Telesinus*, who the Pope called *uir clarissimus*, an honorific title. Gelasius, in fact, said that *Telesinus* had to be considered one of them. This kind of evidence shows a close relationship between a Pope and a Jew, in spite of the persistent anti-Jewish rhetoric. In the other letter Gelasius stated that a Jew was claiming a slave who had escaped, but the slave was arguing that his former owner had circumcised him, a valid reason to escape according to the *Codex Theodosianus*. Complaints about Jews circumcising slaves were common in late antiquity. It is difficult to know with certainty if Jews actually performed circumcision on their slaves, but it is likely that they did, not for a proselytizing aim, but due to ritual necessities. In fact, there are activities such as winemaking or cooking that—according to Jewish law—a non-Jew cannot perform.[14]

Cassiodorus (ca. 485–ca. 585) is another valuable source of information. He served in the administration of Theodoric during the Ostrogothic period. Thanks to him we know that there were Jewish settlements in Genoa and Milan, places where little or no Jewish epigraphy has been found. Concerning Genoa, he mentioned that Theodoric gave permission to reconstruct a synagogue, but the king advised—according to Roman law—that Jews were not permitted to embelish the building (*Variae*, II, 27). A second document was written because Jews petitioned the king to enforce their rights. It is impossible to know which rights had been violated, but the fact is they were suffering aggressions and appealed to Theodoric (*Variae*, IV, 33). In Milan, Jews complained about a certain non-specified problem in their synagogue. Theodoric replied that he guaranteed their rights, but also reminded them that the real faith was Christianity (*Variae*, V, 37). In addition, Cassiodorus stated that a synagogue in the city of Rome had been destroyed. This event, however, is confusing, as the destruction of the synagogue appears to have been a result of a conflict between Jews and their slaves, rather than of a religious conflict (*Variae*, IV, 43).

The *Excerpta Valesiani* are two anonymous chronicles. One of them was written ca. 540 CE and focusses on Theodoric's politics. In relation to the Jews, the chronicle states that a synagogue had been burned in the city of Ravenna. According to the chronicle, the destruction was caused in retaliation against an alleged instance of Jewish disrespect towards holy water (*Excerptum Valesianum II*, XIV, 81–82).[15] The text also alludes to a Jewish officer of Theodoric called Symmachus who ordered the conversion of every Catholic Church to Arianism (*Excerptum Valesianum II*, XVI, 94–95). Again, we can observe a close relationship between a Jew and a Christian king. However, it is important to keep in mind that the chronicle was written as an attack on Theodoric and this entire tale is probably a mere invention with which to besmirch the king's image, associating his Arianism with Judaism. Even though certain historians suggest that Arians were more moderated with regard to Jews, there is no clear evidence pointing to that direction.

The next piece of evidence comes from Procopius of Caesarea (ca. 500–ca. 554), a Byzantine historian, who narrated the Gothic war. According to him, when Belisarius—under Justinian orders—attacked Italy, the Jews of Naples remained loyal to Ostrogothic authorities. The Jewish inhabitants not only helped with the food supply (*De bello Gothico*, V, 8, 41–42) but also defended the city (*De bello Gothico*, V, 10, 24–26). Again, we could see these references as an attempt to discursively associate the Ostrogoths with Jews. Nevertheless, it is highly plausible that Jews defended the city where they lived more or less harmoniously under their Ostrogothic rulers.

Gregory the Great—Pope between 590 and 604 CE—is the most important source with which to reconstruct the history of the Jews in Italy at the end of late antiquity. In fact, Gregory I not only wrote about the Jews in his theological treatises, but also in his letters, compiled in the *Registrum epistularum*. These were practical epistles, written in order to solve religious, political, and social problems.

From them, it is possible to perceive some lived realities of individual Jews and features of Jewish communities.[16]

Of letters relating to Jews, twenty-two out of twenty-six referred to Jews living in Italy. They are mentioned in Agrigento, Cagliari, Luni, Messina, Naples, Palermo, Rome, Terracina, and Venafro. Certain letters only referred to an entire region—such as Sicily—without specifying cities. Luni is the only north Italian city mentioned in connection with Jews. It is true that most of northern Italy was controlled by the Lombards, and as a result the Pope did not send many letters to that region (except for Ravenna, the head of the Byzantine Exarchate). Notwithstanding, we should also bear in mind that the epigraphic evidence is rich in southern and central Italy and scarce in the north.

The Gregorian *Registrum* also shows that some cities, such as Palermo (*Registrum*, VIII, 25), had more than one synagogue. Moreover, the Pope mentioned not only synagogues but also gardens and other structures near them, confirming the existence of synagogal complexes that the Ostia synagogue's remains suggest. Another aspect to remark on is that Jewish communities were interconnected. The Jews of Rome presented petitions to Gregory in the name of the Jewish communities of Marseille, Arles, and Palermo (*Registrum*, I, 45 and VIII, 25). Gregory also stated that Jewish merchants from Naples traveled to Gaul (*Registrum*, VI, 29 and IX, 105). This interconnection is important because it helps us to understand how ideas born in Palestine and Babylonia reached regions as Gaul. It also reveals that a kind of religious uniformity among communities was possible. Iconographical similarities between Bova Marina, Ostia, and synagogues of other regions can be understood in the same way.

The Gregorian *Registrum* also provides information about Jewish economic activities. However, the epistles focus on strategic activities. Minor problems created by an artisan or a peasant were not normally significant enough to attract the attention of regional authorities. There are nine mentions of Jewish economic activities in the *Registrum*: six refer to merchants, two to peasants, and one to landowners.[17] As is known—and the Gregorian epistles confirm—usury was not a Jewish activity until the second millennium (Toch 2013).

Gregory did not provide information about Jewish internal organization. He referred to Jews, but not to rabbis or *archisynagogoi*. As for onomastics, Gregory mentioned twelve Jewish names. Considering that four of them were people who had converted to Christianity and had probably changed their names, just eight remain. The relationship between Semitic and Graeco-Roman names is consistent with the Jewish epigraphic record of the sixth century (Laham Cohen 2013b).

Gregory also provides information about the relationship between Jews and Christians. He stated that the synagogues of Palermo were seized by the local bishop (*Registrum*, VIII, 25 and IX, 38); the Jews of Terracina were twice expelled from their synagogue (*Registrum*, I, 34 and II, 45), and a former Jew who converted to Christianity seized the local synagogue in Cagliari (*Registrum*, IX, 196). In every case, Gregory tried to protect the Jews, suggesting that bishops return the synagogues or, according to the Roman law, gave them a new space with compensation for the damages. He responded in the same protective fashion when the Jews of Naples reported that they had been disturbed by local authorities (*Registrum*, XIII, 13). These situations reveal that attitudes towards Jews were not uniform: some bishops felt that they had to be converted, and others, like Gregory, thought that they should be allowed to continue living, although in subordination, in the Christian world.

Along these same lines, Gregory criticized the forced conversion of the Jews of Gaul (*Registrum*, I, 45), despite also wanting to convert the Jews, albeit with a different strategy. On the one hand, he insisted on converting gradually by preaching. On the other, he instructed his ecclesiastic representatives in Sicily to offer Jews a reduction in their taxes—they were settled on church land—if they accepted Christianity (*Registrum*, II, 50 and V, 7). It is worth mentioning that Gregory only used economic incentives with peasants; merchants were only invited to convert by gradual preaching.

Sometimes Gregory himself acted aggressively towards Jews. When Jews kept Christian slaves, he sent furious letters to ecclesiastical and secular authorities that, against the law, permitted that practice (*Registrum*, III, 37 and IX, 214, among others). He also reacted violently when he discovered that some Roman Christians were keeping the Jewish *Sabbath* (*Registrum*, XIII, 1).[18] All in all, these reactions illustrate that Gregory tolerated Judaism only when he saw it as a static religion instead of an expansive one.

Gregory the Great is a crucial figure in terms of understanding Christian anti-Judaism. In fact, the balanced behaviour displayed in the letters is quite different to his theological writings. In those texts, he repeated the same anti-Jewish tropes that comprised the *adversus Iudaeos* tradition. Why? Because when Gregory wrote his epistles, he was acting politically but when he wrote about Christian theology, he followed the previous line of other Fathers of the Church. He was not schizophrenic, he was a conservative: a Roman politician in his letters and a churchman in his theological treatises and homilies.[19] In spite of this fact, it is important to remember that other members of the Church—even in Italy, and in Gregory's time—acted against the Jews not only discursively but also politically.

In conclusion, there was no systematic policy against Jews in late ancient Italy. Although imperial law subordinated Jews, the real status of each settlement was a result of a network of relationships that involved lay and ecclesiastic authorities. Moreover, the situation of each Jew was conditioned also by his social position, at least on Gregory the Great's *Registrum*: the pressure toward conversion was stronger for Jewish peasants than for Jewish merchants.

Notes

[1] Texts written by pagans on Judaism in late antiquity were collected and commented on by Stern 1980.

[2] Ancient Jewish inscriptions in Rome were gathered by Noy 1995 (= 2 JIWE).

[3] Due to the limited information provided by inscriptions, the prerogatives of each office are not clear. See Van der Horst 2014, 53–56.

[4] Inscriptions from Italy (except Rome), Gaul, and Spain were compiled by Noy 1993 (= 1 JIWE). 1 JIWE n. 86 (early sixth century) mentioned two *rebbites* (sic) that attended a funeral. It is worth noting that in the inscription the reference to rabbis seems to reflect an exceptional situation. We will analyze the controversy about epigraphic rabbis in Chapter 7.

[5] Venusian inscriptions from the ninth century were published in different works. A brief summary can be find in Colafemmina (2000), who has published most of the Jewish Venusian epitaphs.

[6] A פיוט (*piyyut*) is a Jewish liturgical poem that emerged in Palestine ca. sixth century. See Van Bekkum 2008. Cesare Colafemmina had published different southern Italian inscriptions with talmudic references.

[7] The choice of name is not an irrefutable identity marker but does provide clues. On Jewish names in Western Europe during late antiquity, see Ilan 2008.

[8] 2 JIWE n. 277: ζωγράφος (probably a painter); n. 343: *butularus de macello* (probably a butcher); n. 360: Ἔνπορος (sic, with ν) (merchant); n. 341: Ἀρχίατρ[ος] (medic).

[9] There is a current debate around the original use of the building. Some scholars suggest that it was built as a synagogue, while others think that it was originally a house.

[10] On Ostia synagogue, see Olsson et al. 2001, and Levine 2005, 273–78.

[11] *C.тн.* (= *Codex Thedososianus*, Theodosian code) XVI, 8,

25 (423 CE) and XVI, 8, 27 (423 CE). For the text and commentaries on these laws, see Linder 1987, 287–89 and 295–301.

[12] On the synagogue of Bova Marina, see Tromba 2001 and Costamagna 2003.

[13] On Ambrose and the Jews, see Nauroy 2001.

[14] On Christian legislation about Jews and slavery, see De Bonfils 1992.

[15] The chronicle also mentioned a similar event in Rome, but it did not add further information.

[16] On Gregory the Great and the Jews see, among others, Markus 1997, 76–80 and Cohen 1999, 73–94. See also Laham Cohen 2013a.

[17] Merchants or similar (*Registrum,* I, 42; I, 45; I, 66; VI, 29; IX, 105; IX, 40); peasants: (II, 50; V, 7); landowners (IV, 21).

[18] It is worth adding that these Christians could have adopted Jewish practices without the stimulus of Jewish proselytism.

[19] On this topic see Cohen 1999, 73–94. See also Laham Cohen 2013a, 2015a, and 2015b.

Chapter 3

North Africa

In 1937 Stefan Zweig wrote *The Buried Candelabrum,* a short and beautiful novel that recreates the story of the *menorah* of the Second Temple. In fact, the Romans stole the candelabrum after the destruction of Jerusalem in 70 CE. According to Procopius, it was appropriated by the Vandals during the sack of Rome in 455. He also claimed that the *menorah* was taken again by Belisarius and carried to Constantinople when the Vandal kingdom was conquered in 533–534 (*De bello Vandalico*, IV, 9). Subsequently, all trace of the candelabrum was lost. In the novel, Zweig envisioned Jews burying it. The history of the *menorah* is opaque but interesting because it connects three central regions in late antiquity: Italy, North Africa and the Eastern Roman Empire. This chapter is centred on the Jews of North Africa.

Before starting, it is necessary to clarify that Egypt will be analyzed separately. This is not an arbitrary decision: as most scholars recognize, there were great differences—geographical, economical, and cultural—between the North African regions. Furthermore, we will focus on the Roman province of *Africa Proconsularis*, mainly in the city of Carthage and its surroundings, but also Cyrenaica, Numidia, and Mauretania.

Archaeological and epigraphic evidence is scarce. The Naro synagogue (now Hammam-Lif in Tunis, thirty kilometres from Carthage) was discovered in 1883 and was probably built between the fourth and sixth centuries CE. It is the only late ancient synagogue uncovered in Africa.[1] It was a large synagogal complex, comprising more than ten rooms. Moreover, only one chamber can be directly connected to Judaism due to surviving inscriptions and symbols. In fact, two small *menoroth* were found among common North African motifs on the mosaic pavement. Epigraphic evidence found *in situ* confirmed that the building was a synagogue (Le Bohec 1981a, 176–79; Stern 2008, 225–44). Furthermore, lamps decorated with *menoroth* were also found at the site. The building reveals the importance of the local Jewish community and the adoption of ordinary North African—late Roman—art in synagogal decoration. As Karen Stern states, Naro's synagogue shows that Jews, Christians, and pagans used the devotional vocabularies of their immediate environment, incorporating their own particularities (2008, 253).[2]

The epigraphic material—despite being scarce is spread all over North Africa—gives more clues about local Jews.[3] Linguistically, two-thirds of the inscriptions—mostly epitaphs dated between the second and fourth century—were written in Latin, whereas the rest were in Greek and Hebrew. Hebrew inscriptions are not only less numerous than Greek ones, they also showed—like the few found in Rome—a limited use of the language: just the word שלום (*shalom*, peace). In relation to names, the patterns are similar to Rome: Graeco-Roman names are preponderant, at almost 70 per cent.[4] Here we can see again the Romanization of the Jewish population and the adaptation of the Jews to the local milieu. In addition, the structure of the names—*tria nomina*, *dua nomina*, etc.—in Jewish inscriptions changed at the same time as non-Jewish ones (Stern 2008, 99–144).

Gammarth's catacombs (near Carthage) offer an interesting case. Actually, certain scholars such as Stephanie Binder (2012, 19–20) held that those burials proved rabbinical influence on the late ancient Carthaginian Jewish community.[5] The main argument is that the architecture of the catacomb is similar to some Jewish—and clearly rabbinical—catacombs in Palestine, such as Beit She'arim. Nevertheless, the content of the epitaphs are linguistically, iconographically, and onomastically to other Diaspora and non-rabbinical communities, such as the Roman one. On the other hand, no talmudic text was found in Gammarth unlike in southern Italian cities of the early Middle Ages, nor was any direct mention of rabbis found.[6] Furthermore, some inscriptions contain pagan references such as "DM."[7] From our point of view, the Gammarth catacombs should be seen as another Jewish expression in the Diaspora, sharing habits not only with other Jewish communities—in the Land of Israel and outside—but also with non-Jewish groups.[8] The uncovering of a lamp with Christ and a *menorah* also showed the many possibilities of syncretism in late antiquity.[9]

Regarding literary sources, there are references to Carthage in the *Talmud*, but they are generic and do not supply reliable information about North African Jewish communities.[10] Concerning non-Jewish sources, Tertullian (ca. 160–220) is a good starting point. As with the majority of Christian sources, his texts do not openly show contact with Jews. However, they provide hints about the relationship between Jews and Christians in Carthage. The most studied of Tertullian's writing on this topic is, obviously, his *Adversus Iudaeos*. There, Tertullian said that after witnessing a public dispute between a Jew and a Christian, he decided to write a text to demonstrate the superiority of Christianity. As we see again and again in Christian late ancient literature, Tertullian insisted on the idea that Mosaic Law had changed after Jesus. Despite the fact certain authors hold that his view on Judaism was balanced (for example, Binder, 2012), most of Tertullian's production was clearly anti-Jewish.

It is difficult to know if the arguments sustained by Tertullian in his *Adversus Iudaeos* were generated in a real polemic. In fact, while some scholars suggested that Tertullian's text reflects an actual controversy, others argued it was a discursive construction made to reaffirm Christian identity in opposition to Judaism.[11] Ultimately, the fact is that Tertullian wrote a text against the Jews— based on the Old Testament, the only text recognized as valid for both groups—in which he explained why Jesus was the messiah and the Jews had misunderstood him. Even though the text is not especially aggressive, it associated Jews with incredulity. The same tropes are repeated in other Tertullian writings, such as *Ad nationes* or *Apologeticum.* However, it is worth noting that Tertullian's most aggressive words towards the Jews were written in his *Adversus Marcionem.*

In spite of the fact that Tertullian uses a lot of anti-Jewish clichés that only lead us to *hermeneutical* or *rhetorical Jews*, there are some clues about the existence of real contact with Jews. As Claudia Setzer (2006, 73–74) stated, Tertullian knew customs that were not written in the Bible, such as daily immersion or the veiling of women. In addition, William Horbury (1998) suggested that there is a probable reference to a Jewish parody of Jesus' death in *De Spectaculis.*[12] Thus, even though Tertullian occasionally used Jews as rhetorical figures to shape Christian identity, in other cases he revealed certain aspects of *historical Jews*. However, even if Tertullian's texts show some level of knowledge of contemporary Judaism, his information does not help us much to reconstruct the daily life of Jewish communities in North Africa.

Augustine of Hippo (345–430 CE) also authored a text related to Jews: the *Tractatus adversus Iudaeos*, which is actually a sermon. Although the Numidian Hippo (now Annaba in Algeria) was not as important as Carthage, Augustine's production was profuse and his political influence was prominent across the west. The *Tractatus* has been analyzed in depth by several scholars and is not easy to date, but was probably written after 410 CE.[13] It consists of different arguments explaining Jesus' role in God's plan and the Jews' mistaken interpretations of him. Although the text is not very hostile, Augustine repeatedly states, time and again, that Jews cannot understand the Bible and that they are carnal, proud, blind, etc.

Harsher words directed at Jews can be found in other Augustinian texts. As Brent Shaw (2011) has shown, Augustine was strikingly anti-Jewish in his sermons against Donatism. The author clearly exposed Augustine's rhetorical violence towards Jews, highlighting that he was as tough as other Fathers of the Church like Jerome or John Chrysostom. Aggressive expressions related to deicide, among other anti-Jewish topics, are found in different texts written by Augustine, mainly in his works against Christian adversaries. As Shaw stated, Jews in Augustine served as "a useful benchmark of badness" (2011, 286).

The problem of Augustinian texts is, again, that they do not give us any clues about Jews. In fact, *historical Jews* are practically absent from Augustine's works. There are references to them only in two epistles, which is very little compared to the extent of Augustine's literary production. However, it is worth noting that in one of those letters, he ruled in favour of a Jew in a property conflict with a Christian.[14]

Thus, we know that Augustine had contact with Jews, but it is difficult to measure the frequency of the interaction.

Even if we accept that Augustine had knowledge of contemporary Jews, there is an outstanding debate around his position toward Jews. The traditional point of view emphasizes aggression towards Judaism motivated by the competition between Jewish and Christian orthodoxies (Efroymson 2009). But Paula Fredriksen (2008, among other publications) takes a different approach. First, she considers that Augustine's attitude towards the Jews was relatively benign. Second, she maintains that position was a product of Augustine's discussions with other Christian groups, mainly the Manicheans. As Marcion (ca. 85–ca. 160), Manicheans denied the value of the Old Testament as a sacred book. Augustine responded to them by restoring the role of the Jews before Jesus as the chosen people, but also after Christ as *testes veritatis* (witnesses of the truth).[15]

Fredriksen's position was both criticized and praised. A full discussion of her conclusions is beyond the scope of this volume, but it is worth remembering that her work is insightful and has promoted a radical re-reading of Augustine's perspective towards Judaism. Nevertheless, Augustine's texts show more about his attitude toward Judaism than about Jews in North Africa.

Augustine died in 430 CE during the Vandal siege. The next piece of information about Jews in North Africa came not from Vandals but from Byzantines, after the conquest of Belisarius in 533.[16] Indeed, the *Novella 37 de Africana Ecclesia* established that all the synagogues of Africa had to be converted to churches. Unfortunately, there is no information to confirm the fulfillment of the law, which was probably an isolated decree, produced immediately after the Byzantine conquest (Rabello 1988 and Linder 1987, 381–89).

Notes

[1] There were controversies around a building in Leptis Magna which was identified as a synagogue (Hachlili 1998, 53–58). However, no definitive proof of the identification was provided. On the other hand, Lund (1995) referred to a probable synagogue in Carthage due to the uncovering of many lamps decorated with *menoroth* in the same area. His theory, however, is highly speculative.

[2] On the Hammam-Lif synagogue, see Hachlili 1998, 47–49, Levine 2005, 279–81, and Bleiberg 2015.

[3] The compilation of North African inscriptions made by Le Bohec 1981a is still useful.

[4] Le Bohec 1981b. See also Stern 2008. However, comparatively there are more Semitic names in North Africa than in Rome. This was occasionally explained as the combination of the influence of other Semitic languages, such as Punic, and the effect of a close relationship with Jewish—and rabbinical—communities of Palestine. Nevertheless, as we will see later in this chapter, this last point is controversial. On the other hand, the difference between Rome and North Africa—15 per cent more Semitic names—is not significant.

[5] Also Le Bohec (1981a) associated Gammarth's catacombs with rabbinical Judaism.

[6] Only one North African inscription (Le Bohec 1981a, n. 80), in Volubilis—in present-day Morocco—mentions a rabbi. The debate around epigraphic rabbis is dealt with below.

[7] DM—Dis Manibus—was a pagan formula habitually employed in epitaphs. However, it was also found in Christian and Jewish contexts. There is a current debate around its Christian and Jewish use. Did it just appear as a result of reutilization of previous gravestones? Were tombstones prefabricated in shared workshops? Did it have religious connotations? The answer is not simple.

[8] This is also the position of Stern (2008) and was challenged by Binder (2012, 19–20).

[9] See Simon 1978. As the *menorah* is inverted in the *lucerna*, certain scholars suggested that it represented the subordination of the Jewish religion instead of syncretism.

[10] For example, *y* (= *Yerushalmi, Jerusalem Talmud*) Yoma 39a; *b* (= *Bavli, Babylonian Talmud*) Berakhot 33a; *b Rosh Hashana*, 26a.

[11] On Tertullian's *Adversus Iudaeos* see, among others, Efroymson 1979, Dunn 2008, and Binder 2012.

[12] In *De spectaculis* 30, 5-6 Tertullian—arguing against Jews—suggested that they claimed Mary was a prostitute and Jesus' corpse had been moved by a gardener (instead of being resurrected). As Horbury (1998) correctly suggested, even though both references could have been interpretations of the New Testament, Mary's morality is also attacked in the *Bavli* and the gardener moving Jesus' corpse is found in the literature known as *Toledot Yeshu*: parodies on Jesus' life and death that were popular among Jews in late antiquity, the Middle Ages, and even in modern times. The first manuscripts of *Toledot Yeshu* (dating from the ninth century) were found in the Cairo *Genizah*, but Christian authors such as Origen, Epiphanius and, later, Agobard, knew about those parodies. The exact dating of the *Toledot Yeshu* literature remains controversial. On *Toledot Yeshu*, see Meerson and Schäfer 2014.

[13] According to Shaw (2011, 281), the *Adversus Iudaeos* was written in the last year or two of Augustine's life.

[14] Augustine, *Epistolae*, *8. There, Augustine mediated in a conflict between a Jewish landowner named Licinius and Victor, probably a fellow bishop. Interestingly, Licinius had visited Augustine to obtain help. The other communication is epistle 71, where Augustine—subtly arguing against Jerome—affirmed that the Jews of Oea (present-day Tripoli) were consulted, regarding their Hebrew knowledge, about Jerome's translation of the book of Jonah. It is difficult to know if this information is real or just a polemical argument. A Jewish healer is mentioned in *De civitate Dei,* 22, 8.

[15] On the Jews as *testes veritatis*, see Cohen 1999, 19-66, and Massie 2011.

[16] Also Quodvultdeus wrote against Jews. However, only *hermeneutical* and *rhetorical Jews* are found in his texts.

Chapter 4

Gaul

No more than three lamps decorated with *menoroth* were found in ancient Gaul, representing the entire late ancient Jewish archeological record in the region (Boddens Hosang 2010, 127-28). In addition, only three inscriptions were discovered. Among them, one—the most important, an epitaph that will be analyzed in the following chapter—pertained to the western region of the *Gallia Narbonensis*, under Visigothic control. The others were a seal with the name *Ianuarius* and a *menorah* (*1 Jewish Inscriptions of Western Europe* (= 1 JIWE) n. 190), and a ring that contained the name *Asterius* and two *menoroth* (1 JIWE n. 192).[1] It is worth noting that the ring and seal could have belonged to people just traveling in Gaul (Handley 2000, 239-54). Once again, we need non-Jewish sources.[2]

The first reference to Jews in a Gallic source comes from Ravennius (*d.* ca. 461 CE), Archbishop of Arles, who stated that Jews attended Hilary of Arles' (ca. 401-449) funeral and sang—in Hebrew—in his honour (*Vita Hilarii Arelatensis* 22, 29). There are several stories about Jews mourning and honouring Christian bishops in the period. Even though it is not impossible that Jews could have had a good relationship with a bishop, the most probable hypothesis is that these kinds of narratives were intended to glorify the saints' image.[3] For that reason, information provided about singing in Hebrew has to be approached with caution.

With Sidonius Apollinaris (ca. 430–489 CE), bishop of Arles, we are on firmer ground. He mentioned Jews and former Jews converted to Christianity in his letters. In fact, despite criticizing his Judaism, he commended a Jew called *Gozolas* in two epistles.[4]

However, in Gaul there were also churchmen who vilified Judaism from the beginning of late antiquity. For example, Hilary of Poitiers (ca. 310–367 CE) repeatedly condemned Jews from a theological point of view. In Hilary, Jews functioned merely as hermeneutical devices to construct and transmit Christian identity. In fact, we do not know if he actually interacted with Jews. The same applies to Prosper of Aquitaine (ca. 390–463 CE).[5]

Evidence concerning Jewish communities comes mostly from the Merovingian period. The Merovingian dynasty reigned for nearly three hundred years and was characterized by continuous territorial disputes between heirs. Caesarius of Arles (ca. 470–542 CE), who lived in a volatile Arles—which passed between the rule of Visigoths, Ostrogoths, and Franks—delivered more than 250 sermons. He also employed Jews as rhetorical devices. Though he was aggressive toward Judaism, his discourses were milder than other churchmen. Contemporary sources suggest, once again, that Jews grieved for him when he died, but this is probably an example of the continuation of the aforementioned trope about the death of saints.[6]

Caesarius presided over the Council of Agde in 506. Councils are another type of source that reveal, albeit tangentially, interaction between Jews and Christians in Gaul (Pakter 1988; Boddens Hosang 2010). The council decided that Jews had to be catechumens for eight months before conversion (canon 34). In addition, canon 40 stated that meals with Jews were forbidden.

Before the Council of Agde, another council was held in Vannes, around 465 CE. Canon 12 prohibited clerics from eating with Jews, arguing that they considered Christian food impure. During 517 CE, a council held in *Epaon* again forbade Christians from sharing meals with Jews. Other prohibitions of shared meals are found in canon 14 of the Third Council of Orleans (538 CE), and canon 15 of the Council of Mâcon (585 CE). Does this indicate that Christians were eating alongside Jews? Or were councils simply repeating previous prohibitions? Answering that is not easy, but the most probable hypothesis is that Christians and Jews were having meals together because they did not understand the difference or they just did not attribute any importance to their neighbour's religion. The boundaries between Jewish and Christian identities were clear only for religious elites, not for the lay population.

With regard to mixed marriages, they were forbidden in canon 19 of the Second Council of Orleans (533 CE). Again, bishops were trying to separate communities.[7] The same prohibition was enunciated two years later at Clermont-Ferrand (canon 6). Canon 9 of the same council also established that Jews were not permitted to be judges over Christians, a prohibition that had been promulgated previously in the *Codex Theodosianus* (XVI, 8, 16 and XVI, 8, 24). In canon 14 of the Third Council of Orleans (538 CE), another prohibition against mixed marriages was enacted. In the same canon, there is a limitation that had been already imposed in Imperial Law: interdiction of ownership of Christian slaves by Jews. Nevertheless, the canon was milder because it established that the Jews should receive a *competens pretium* (suitable price) for the lost slave. Regarding this issue, the situation of the Jews gradually worsened. Thus, while in the Third Council of Orleans, a Christian slave was only able to abandon his Jewish owner when the Jew had beaten him; in canon 30 of the Fourth

Council of Orleans (541 CE) no reason was necessary for freeing a Christian slave. Moreover, in 585 CE, canon 16 of the Council of Mâcon stated a fixed compensation—12 *solidi*—for each Christian slave freed. The sum was worse than the "suitable price" stipulated in previous councils because, according to William Pakter (1988, 90), it was lower than the normal market price.

Above, when we analyzed the letter written by Pope Gelasius, we stated that Jews tended to convert their slaves. The same preoccupation was also seen in Gregory the Great's epistles. Canon 31 of the Fourth Council of Orleans and canon 17 of Mâcon referred explicitly to Jewish proselytism towards slaves and established penalties against the practice.

Finally, canon 33 of the Third Council of Orleans is particularly interesting. It prohibited Jews from being present among Christians between Holy Thursday and Easter Monday. Was this law an anti-Jewish measure? Or, perhaps, were rulers trying to avoid attacks that were regularly directed against Jews during Easter? Both answers are possible. From our point of view, the authorities were attempting to avoid public disorder during a period in which, in several churches, Christians heard that the Jews had killed Christ.[8]

All in all, the councils offer a tool with which to reconstruct the interaction between Jews and Christians. It is true that no direct conclusions can be drawn from religious law. Certainly, the prohibition of shared meals does not mechanically imply that Jews and Christians were eating together. Nevertheless, the repetition of that law could signify that the authorities were worried about the practice.

The most widely known event related to Judaism in late ancient Gaul is the forced conversion of the Jews of Clermont-Ferrand in 576 CE. There are two sources which narrate the episode: a *carmen* written by Venantius Fortunatus (ca. 530–ca. 600 CE) and *Libri historiarum* by Gregory of Tours (ca. 538–594 CE). Venantius wrote the poem due to a specific request from Gregory, who related the facts to him. Thus, Venantius' poem relies on information provided by the bishop of Tours. Nevertheless, the accounts are slightly different.

Venantius' *carmen* is particularly aggressive. He employed *adversus Iudaeos* tropes continuously. He even spoke about a Jewish smell, a reference that is not found in previous Christian writings. According to the poem (*Carmina*, V) the events unfolded as follows: during Ascension Day, without any reason, Christians destroyed Clermont's synagogue; the local bishop, Avitus, gave a violent speech trying to convert the Jews of the city; the Jews resisted and gathered in a house; an armed Christian mob then threatened the Jews; the Jews sent a messenger to Avitus affirming that they agreed to be converted, and after that the whole Jewish community converted to Christianity.

Gregory of Tours laid out a different version. The first attack, in his tale, came from the Jews. During Easter—again, at Easter[9]—a Jew poured rancid oil over another Jew who was going to be converted to Christianity and was marching in white garments in the middle of the Christian procession. The Christians reacted immediately but Avitus decided to calm them. From here, Gregory repeats Venantius' narrative with, however, two differences: no weapons are used by the Christians and not all the Jewish community were converted. Walter Goffart (1989, 308) correctly stated that Gregory "could not quite stomach the armed crowd" and opted for the idea of a non-violent conversion. Along the same lines is the affirmation that only five hundred Jews of the community were converted and the rest went to Marseille. Indeed, Gregory of Tours, as with Gregory the Great and

Isidore of Seville, felt that conversions had to be voluntary. Even though sometimes they acted in contradiction with this idea, their texts sustained the need for sincere conversion.

It is difficult to decide which version is more accurate. Nevertheless, the fact is that in 576 the bulk of the Jewish community of Clermont was forcibly converted (Goffart 1989; Rose 2002). This was not common for the period and it is important to highlight the decision came from Avitus and not from lay authorities. As was pointed out in the Italian context, local decisions could change the fortune of each Jewish community.

But Avitus' resolution needs to be compared with other actions that affected the life of the Jews in late ancient Gaul. According to his anonymous hagiographer, Ferréol of Uzès (ca. 530–581 CE) forcibly converted the Jewish community of Uzès at some point between 575 and 581 CE. In 582, according to Gregory of Tours, King Chilperic I (ca. 539–584 CE) decided that Jews must be converted to Christianity. As we saw, Gregory the Great—in 591—denounced that Jews from Marseille and Arles were being converted by force. Finally, the *Chronicle of Fredegar* (ca. seventh century) stated that King Dagobert (ca. 603–639) decreed the conversion of the entire Jewish community of Gaul in 632–633.

Obviously, these facts paint a dismal picture for the Jewish communities of Gaul at the end of late antiquity. However, scholars have different perspectives on the impact of each measure. Regarding Ferréol, only one source, the *Vita Ferreoli*, mentions the conversion. Concerning Chilperic's decision, Gregory of Tours was not very clear and he was probably referring, as we will see, to the conversion of certain Jews. With regard to Dagobert, only the controversial *Chronicle of Fredegar* spoke about the forced conversion and many scholars doubted the veracity of the event or its real scope.

Certainly, it is difficult to deny that the situation of the Jews in late ancient Gaul was problematic. Scholars such as Michel Rouche (2003) are convinced that all the mentioned actions against the Jews were actually performed. Nevertheless, the information that we have is fragmentary.

What do we know about Jewish daily life in late ancient Gaul? As suggested, Gallic councils present useful information. Additionally, Gregory of Tours provided some hints about them. Even though Judaism and Jews were not his primary concern, some of Gregory's tales include Jews. The bishop described the story of Priscus, a merchant close to King Chilperic. Priscus had a discussion about religion with the king, who called on Gregory to convince and convert him. But the Jew was not converted, and he even argued against the king and the bishop. In fact, Priscus deployed anti-Christian arguments (*Libri Historiarum*, VI, 5).[10] Nonetheless, as has already been noted, Chilperic decreed that certain Jews, including Priscus, must be converted to Christianity. Priscus resisted again, but this time he was imprisoned. When he obtained a special permit—by bribe—to attend the marriage of his son, he was killed by a former Jew—who had converted to Christianity—called Pathir (*Libri Historiarum*, VI, 17).

It is very difficult to find out more about Priscus because Gregory is the only available source. Moreover, his example shows the proximity of certain Jews to royal power, and the risks that position entailed. In addition, we must bear in mind that Jews carried out different economic activities in late antiquity but, as we saw in the Italian case, the sources focus on people in high positions such as Priscus, not ordinary workers.

Gregory also mentioned that when Guntram (ca. 532–592 CE) arrived in Orleans, Jews asked him to reconstruct their synagogue (*Libri Historiarum*, VIII, 1). The king rejected the idea and, also, gave a speech attacking the Jews. This reference is important for two reasons. First, a synagogue was destroyed in the kingdom, showing tensions between Jews and Christians, even though it is impossible to identify the perpetrator (clerics? lay people? local authorities?). Second, the Jews—continuing the tradition of the *Codex Theodosianus*—attempted to convince Guntram, and that fact reveals a community that thought negotiation was possible.

Other fragments of Gregory of Tours' texts show peaceful coexistence between Jews and Christians. For example, the predecessor of Avitus of Clermont, Cautinus, was said to be a friend of the Jews (*Libri Historiarum*, IV, 12). Of course, Gregory could have tried to denigrate the bishop's image, associating him with Judaism. *Libri Historiarum* also presented a tale of an archdeacon who, after partially recovering his sight in St. Martin's sanctuary, appealed to a Jewish doctor for a complete cure and—as a divine punishment—lost his vision. The story was probably an invention but shows, again, the possibility of interaction.[11] Gregory also mentioned a ship manned by Jews, displaying the diversity of occupations held by Jews in the period (*De gloria confessorum*, 95).

In conclusion, the situation of the Jews in Gaul can be interpreted in different ways. There was violence, expressed by forced conversions and destruction of synagogues. On the other hand, there is evidence of interaction between Jews and Christians, not only among lay people but also public officials and churchmen. Again, the fate of each Jewish community depended on the king in power and local bishops. No systematic policy to the detriment of Jews was carried out, except the controversial decree of Dagobert. Centuries later, Agobard of Lyon (ca. 779–840 CE) under the Carolingians complained about Jews collecting taxes or converting slaves. Although Agobard wrote for the purposes of polemic, the most probable explanation is that Jewish communities led a relatively normal life in Gaul, even after Dagobert.[12]

Notes

[1] 1 JIWE n. 189, from Auch, seems to be a late inscription.

[2] On the first traces of Jews in Gaul, see Geisel 1998.

[3] Also Gregory of Tours (*Vitae Patrum*, 6, 7) said that Gall, another Christian bishop, was also mourned by the Jews at his funeral.

[4] Sidonius Apollinaris, *Epistulae et carmina*, III, 4 and IV, 5. Mentions of other Jews also in VI, 11. References to a Christian converted from Judaism, in VIII, 13.

[5] On these authors see González Salinero 2000a.

[6] On Caesarius and the Jews, see Mikat 1996. The Jewish reaction at his funeral was narrated in *Vita Caesarii* (2, 4, 35), composed by five bishops, including Cyprianus of Toulon (ca. 517–545 CE). The *Vita* (1, 3, 22) also affirmed that Jews betrayed the Merovingians during a siege of Arles.

[7] Also the *Codex Theodosianus* (*c.th.* XVI, 8, 6 and *c.th.* III, 7, 2) had forbidden marriages between Jews and Christians.

[8] Canon 14 of Mâcon council repeated the same law.

[9] It is important to remark on the usual violence against Jews during Easter in late antiquity. Easter violence was even more intense in the Middle Ages.

[10] Priscus, provocatively, stated that God had no descendants nor partners. He quoted the Old Testament (*Dt.* 32, 39) to justify his position.

[11] *Libri Historiarum.* V, 6. In *De virtutibus sancti Martini episcopi* (III, 50), Gregory referred to a Jew who mocked a Christian for believing in the curative capabilities of Saint Martin's relics. The Christian was healed and the Jew fell ill, sticking to his Judaism due to stubbornness.

[12] On Agobard of Lyon and the Jews, see Heil 1998 and Langenwalter 2010. As we stated previously, Agobard knew certain tales contained in *Toledot Yeshu*. See n. 12 (Chapter 3).

Chapter 5

Spain

At some point between 612 and 616,[1] Sisebut (ca. 565-621 CE), King of the Visigoths, decreed that all the Jews of the kingdom had to be converted to Christianity. After that decision, both religious and secular law repeatedly discussed the new situation. But the legislation was ambiguous. It is frequently unclear whom the laws were referring to when using the term "Jew": whether they were former Jews converted to Christianity or, simply, Jews. Furthermore, Visigothic legislation never referred to ex-Jews as "Christians" or "new Christians." That vagueness could be seen even in the Seventeenth Council of Toledo (694 CE) that established the enslavement of the "Jews" of the realm.[2] Were they Jews or were they Christians? As we will see, the actual extent of forced conversions in the Visigothic world is difficult to establish.

Was the Visigothic policy toward Judaism an exception? The majority of scholarship on the issue would answer in the affirmative but there is not a uniform consensus on the topic. As was noted in the previous chapter, there were forced conversions in Gaul. We also find forced conversions in the east. However, the magnitude of the measures against Jews and former Jews in Spain was on a different scale. For almost one hundred years laws against *Iudaei* and *Iudaei baptizati*[3] were promulgated by councils

and kings. There was no precedent of this kind of attitude against the Jews in antiquity and because of that,
Visigothic *Hispania* should be considered an exception.

As previously mentioned, the extent of the forced
conversions must be analyzed carefully. First, the law
continued to speak about groups of non-converted Jews
until the end of the seventh century. Second, due to the
existence of certain texts written by Christians that, even
after the Sisebut decree, attacked Jewish practices and
beliefs. In addition, there is a Jewish epitaph written during
Egica's rule.

Before analyzing the seventh century, it is necessary
to return to the first testimonies on late ancient Hispanic
Jews. Unfortunately, few inscriptions have been found
(1 JIWE nn. 177–189) related to Judaism in late ancient Spain
and only one of them was written after the forced conversion (1 JIWE n. 189). It is an inscription ordered by a Jew
called *Paragoro* for his three dead children in Narbonne. It
was dated explicitly in the reign of Egica, written in Latin,
with some words in Hebrew and a *menorah*. This is very
important because, more than 70 years after the Sisebut
forced conversion, there were Jews living in a territory
controlled by Visigoths. The only problem with this inscription is that it was found in Narbonne. The west of *Gallia
Narbonensis* was under Visigothic rule but control of that
area was not easy for the monarchy. In fact, the enslavement of Jews established in the Seventeenth Council
of Toledo included an exception for the *Narbonensis*.
Beforehand, Julian of Toledo had said that region was
the "brothel of the Jews."[4] For this reason, the Narbonne
inscription should be considered with caution.

Archaeologically, the panorama is not better. There was
an intense debate about a building found in Elche. When
it was uncovered in 1905, it was generally deemed to be
a church. Nevertheless, some authors stated that it was a

synagogue. Nowadays, even though there is no definitive consensus, most scholars believe that the building was Christian. Because of that, it will not be analyzed here.[5]

The earlier late ancient texts about the Jewish presence in *Hispania* come from the Council of Elvira (ca. 304 CE).[6] Canons of that council that referred to Jews reflected a close relationship with Christians: canon 16 prohibited marriage between a Christian woman and a Jew, and canon 78 condemned adultery between a Christian man and a Jewish woman. Canon 49 forbade Jewish blessings of Christian fields, and canon 50 rejected shared meals. If the abovementioned date is accepted for this council, Hispanic bishops of the early fourth century were worried—as can be seen in the Gallic case—about possible influences of Judaism on Christians.

As Raul González Salinero (2015) showed, Gregory of Elvira (fourth century) expressed the same kind of tension. In his homilies, the bishop suggested that there were open disputes between Jews and Christians. Gregory struck an aggressive stance towards Judaism, employing *adversus Iudaeos* tropes. He also emphasized the risks of practices such as *Sabbath* and circumcision.[7]

Sometimes anti-Jewish discourse was accompanied by physical violence. This is the case narrated in the Letter of Severus of Minorca—also known as *Epistula Severi*—a document dating from the fifth century. The *Epistula* describes the miraculous (and violent) conversion of the Jewish community of Mahón, a city on the island of Minorca, ca. 418 CE. According to the letter, the relationship between Christians and Jews deteriorated after the arrival of the relics of Saint Stephen. The tension came to a climax when Jewish women attacked a Christian procession that was trying to initiate a public confrontation with the Jews. The Christian retaliation—according to the *Epistula*—was the destruction of the local synagogue. This event triggered—after other tensions—the wholesale conversion of the Jewish community, including members who had held public office as *defensor civitatis* and *Patronus*. This last fact is important because it shows that Jews holding public offices was usual in the late ancient world.

The incident in Mahón bears strong similarities with the forced conversion of the Jews of Clermont. Unfortunately, there are no further sources that would allow greater precision on the issue. Nevertheless, the facts narrated by Severus are plausible (Bradbury 1996; Sivan 2013).

But as we observed previously, forced conversions were not always the rule. A very interesting example, also on Visigothic territory, was canon 9 of the Council of Narbonne (589 CE). It stated that Jews were allowed to hold a funeral procession through the city, but they were forbidden to sing psalms (Linder 1997, 475–78). That norm expressed the place reserved for Judaism in certain bishops' minds: a marginal and silent subsistence.[8]

Continuing with religious law, another council was held in 589: the Third Council of Toledo. This meeting was vital, because it was celebrated after Reccared's (ca. 559–601) rejection of Arianism and the conversion of the kingdom to the Nicene faith. Canon 14 against Judaism was in line with both lay and religious antecedents: prohibition of mixed marriages, ownership of Christian slaves, public office, circumcision, etc. There is only one new addition to the canon, a dramatic one: children born to mixed marriages had to be taken from their families and baptized. There is still a fierce debate around the impact of Reccared's conversion to the Nicene Creed on the relationship between Jews and Christians (González Salinero 2002). However, from our point of view, the real change came with the forced conversion decreed by Sisebut.

Unfortunately, there are no records of Sisebut's decree. It was mentioned in the Fourth Council of Toledo (633 CE) and there are references in *Historia Gothorum,* 60, and in *Etymologiae* V, 39, 42, both texts written by Isidore of Seville (ca. 560–636). When Isidore explained Sisebut measure he said that it was taken with zeal but without wisdom because faith had to be obtained with persuasion and not violence. Also in his *Sententiae* (II, 2, 4), Isidore stated that arguments and *exempla* and not force were the best ways to convert people. Nevertheless, he probably presided over the Fourth Council of Toledo, where canon 57 stipulated the impossibility of reverting the forced conversion. Despite accepting the inappropriate nature of forced conversions, the canon prohibited the new converts from returning to Judaism. This measure can be seen as theological realism—conversion is permanent—or as a tacit endorsement of the monarchy's policy.

In fact, Isidore's attitude towards Judaism was harsh. References to Jews and Judaism can also be found in his theological works. Furthermore, he wrote an entire treatise dedicated to Judaism: *De fide catholica contra Iudaeos.* The text lacked originality: it repeated all the *adversus Iudaeos* tropes of previous Fathers of the Church (even *anti-Donatist* arguments employed by Augustine) and it did not provide any information about contemporary Jews. Moreover, it is significant that Isidore decided to write a text against the Jews. Even though it is difficult to date the work with precision, it is probable that he wrote the book after the forced conversion, with the aim of convincing and retaining the new converts to Christianity.[9]

Certain scholars, such as Bat-Sheva Albert (1990, 214–15), have suggested that Isidore's intention was the gradual elimination of Judaism. Nevertheless, that statement has to be approached cautiously. Isidore, like the majority of the church fathers, wanted the conversion of the Jews. In that sense, he was similar to other churchmen. However, he lived in a different context, where the Visigothic monarchy had decided to use violence to convert Jews *en masse*. He adapted himself to the situation. Thus, he was no more or less violent than Gregory the Great or Gregory of Tours.[10]

Isidore was not the last late ancient Hispanic churchman who spoke about Visigothic "Jews". There are references in Braulius of Zaragoza (ca. 590–651 CE), Taius of Zaragoza (ca. 600–683), and Ildefonsus of Toledo (ca. 607–667). Unfortunately, none of the three provided information about Jewish daily life. They simply repeated anti-Jewish tropes without mentioning interaction between Jews and Christians. In certain fragments they suggested that "Jews" had continued with their perfidy, but it is not clear which group they were speaking about; non-converted Jews or Christians who had formerly been Jews.[11] Only Julian of Toledo (ca. 642–690 CE) gave certain hints about Jews and former Jews. For example, in *De comprobatione aetatis sextae* he seemed to be familiar with certain rabbinical traditions.[12] In addition, in *Historia Wambae*, as we noted previously, he disapproved of the Visigothic policy in Narbonne towards Jews. All in all, Christian authors do not offer much help in the analysis of the Hispanic "Jewish" communities in the seventh century.

In fact, there is a problematic dependence on legal sources, both religious and secular. As we said previously, it is difficult to know with precision whether a law appeared in order to solve a problem or if it was a preventive measure. Furthermore, the repetition of a law could signify a simple juridical custom or the persistence of the problem that previous laws aimed to resolve. Additionally, as we anticipated, Visigothic law regarding Jews has another problem. The word *Iudaeus* is used both for Jews and for Christians who had previously been Jews. Sometimes it is easy to identify the groups the legislation was referring to, as in *Lex Visigothorum* (=*LV*) 12, 2, 10,[13] where it is written "Jews" in opposition to "baptized Jews", or in *LV.* 12, 2, 18, where "Jews" have to avoid contact with the "other Jews that persevere in their perfidy of their heart and neglect the conversion to the Christian faith." But in other laws, discerning whether "Jew" denotes a Jew or a Christian is not easy (Benveniste 2006; Laham Cohen and Pecznik 2016).

However, if the usefulness of the legislation as a historical source is accepted,[14] a model can be suggested. After the Sisebut decree, lawmakers insisted on two core policies: control of formerly Jewish Christians and conversion of Jews. Regarding control, there are many laws, but we will present the most important: Former Jews were compelled to pronounce personal and public oaths where they had to state their abandonment of Judaism and acceptance of Christianity (*LV.* 12, 2, 17 and 12, 3, 14). They had to remain with the local bishop during *Sabbath* and other Jewish celebrations (*LV.* 12, 3, 20), and they had to publically observe Christian festivities (*LV.* 12, 3, 6). When they travelled, they had to obtain a letter from the local bishop of every town where they had stayed (*LV.* 12, 3, 20). They could not provide testimony in a trial (*LV* 12, 2, 10). They also had to eat pork.[15]

Thus, according to the law, ex-Jews were treated as suspicious by the authorities. We do not know to what extent the legislation was actually enforced, but symbolically Jewishness was thought of as some kind of indelible mark. A *Iudaeus baptizatus* was neither a *Christianus*, nor a *Iudaeus*.

The law also referred to Jews who had never been baptized. This shows that the conversion process was not fully accomplished. Nevertheless, lawmakers tried, repeatedly, to complete conversions. Visigothic legislation also punished Christians—even inside religious and lay elites—who collaborated with the Jews (*LV.* 12, 3, 24, among others), revealing, probably, the integration of the "Jews" into society.[16]

Religious law was similar, but less systematic than secular. As with the laic law, it established that Jews had to be converted, and Christians—former Jews, also called "Jews"—had to persevere in their Christian faith. Suspicion towards this group was—also in the canons—perpetual.[17]

Why were Jews mass converted in *Hispania*? Why, after the failure of the Sisebut decree, did other kings continue attempting to convert Jews and control them? The answers are not straightforward. It is likely that the Visigothic monarchy thought religious conversion was the best way to solidify the union of a weak and multiethnic kingdom. The Visigoth kings, in fact, were in an insecure position because Visigoth nobility was never entirely controlled by the regnant houses. However, other kingdoms were as volatile as the Visigoth and they did not choose religious unification as a solution. Putting historiographic points of contention to one side, the important issue in the Visigoth case is that, for first time in Europe, the entire Jewish population of one kingdom was converted by force and, after that, there was a permanent policy of maintaining the new *status quo.* It was also the first time when even after conversion, former Jews continued to be considered "Jews."

Notes

[1] There are different opinions around the precise date of the forced conversion. We follow González Salinero (2000b, 28), who opted for 616 due to the *Etymologies* of Isidore of Seville, among other reasons.

[2] Canon 8. See council texts and commentaries, in Martínez Díez and Rodriguez 1992, and Linder 1997.

[3] There are rules in Visigothic law, in which certain activities were prohibited for "Jews" and "baptized Jews". For example, *LV*

12.2.10 stated: *Merito ergo testificari prohibiti sunt Iudei, seu baptizati, sive non extiterint baptizati.*

[4] Julian of Toledo, *Historia Wambae*, 5. In *Insultatio*, I, Julian criticized the population of the *Narbonensis* for nurturing friendship with the Jews.

[5] A summary of the different positions, in Poveda Navarro 2014. See also Levine 2005, 281–83.

[6] Also known as the Council of Iliberris. Although the majority of scholars agree on the existence of the council and its approximate dating, certain researchers have doubts about the council text that survived to the present day. See, for example, Vilella—Barreda 2002.

[7] Similar expressions can be found in Potamius of Lisbon (fourth century) and Pacian of Barcelona (ca. 310–ca. 388). On these authors, see González Salinero 2015.

[8] Interestingly, the Bishop of Terracina said to Gregory the Great that he had expelled the Jews from the synagogue because the building was too close to the church and the psalms could be heard from it. See Gregory the Great, *Registrum*, II, 45.

[9] This point, however, remains controversial. Certain authors, in fact, consider that the *De Fide* was written before the Sisebut decree of forced conversion (González Salinero 2000b, 121–23). There are also discussions around the degree of knowledge that Isidore had of Judaism.

[10] On Isidore and the Jews, see also Albert 1990, Cohen 1999, 95–122, Drews 2006, and Laham Cohen 2010.

[11] On these authors, see Blumenkranz 1963, Del Valle Rodríguez 1998, and González Salinero 2015.

[12] There are doubts around the religion of Julian. Indeed, a Mozarab Chronicle written in 754 stated that he had been a Jew. Concerning rabbinical traditions, Julian wrote about the cosmic *Sabbath*, a messianic idea that has similarities with *b Sanhedrin* 97. On Julian, see Del Valle Rodriguez 1998.

[13] Even though Visigoths never referred to their laws as *Lex Visigothorum* (*LV*), we will use Zeumer's (1902) compilation and terminology.

[14] Rachel Stocking (2008) argues that the information about Jews and *conversi* which can be obtained from Visigothic law is not valid because it dealt more with lawgivers' conceptions than with the reality.

[15] It is very interesting that laws compelling Jews to eat pork show changes even inside the Visigoth law. *LV.* 12, 2, 8 stated that

Jews had to eat everything, without discerning between pure and impure food. *LV.* 12, 2, 17 expressed that "Jews" had to swear—it was a *placitum*—that they ate pork but if they were not able, at least to consume food cooked with pork. *LV* 12, 3, 7, the last law regarding pork consumption, stated that if "Jews" were not able to eat pork because they felt aversion due to the nature of the pig meat, but they acted as Christians, they did not need to be punished. In this law, we think is possible to see a kind of nego-tiation between the recently converted and the authorities. See Laham Cohen and Pecznik 2016.

[16] On Jews and Visigothic law, see González Salinero 2000b, and Martin-Nemo-Pekelman 2008.

[17] As we stated, there are similarities between secular and religious law regarding the "Jews". In fact both *corpora* mutually influenced each other. Fourth Council of Toledo, 633 CE: against Christians that collaborate with "Jews" (c. 58); children of the "Jews" had to be separated from their parents in order to be educated by Christians (c. 60); prohibition of interaction between "Jews that were converted" and "Jews that persist in their Judaism" (c. 62); against "Jewish" ownership of Christian slaves (c. 66). Sixth Council of Toledo, 638 CE: public oath made by "Jews" abjuring Judaism (c. 3). Ninth Council of Toledo, 655 CE: "Baptized Jews" must remain with bishops during the days of Jewish festivities (c. 7). There are also general references to the "Jews" and confirmation of previous laws in the Eight (653 CE), Tenth (656 CE), Twelfth (681 CE), Sixteenth (693 CE), and Seventeenth (694 CE) Councils of Toledo.

Chapter 6

Egypt

It is known that Alexandria was probably the most important Jewish diasporic settlement in antiquity. In fact both Jewish and non-Jewish sources referred to a huge Jewish population in the coastal city. However, it was not only Alexandria that was important; Jews were spread all over Egypt. Several texts written by Jews living in Egypt survived. The most widely known author is, obviously, Philo (Hadas-Lebel 2012), but there are also anonymous sources such as the *Epistle of Aristeas* (Nickelsburg 2005). The *Epistle* narrated the mythical translation of the Old Testament into Greek, associating the *Septuagint* to Alexandria.[1] But these writings were produced before the second century CE. Unfortunately, in late antiquity there are fewer Jewish (and non-Jewish) sources that spoke about Jews. Why could that be?

Life for Jews in Egypt had three turning points: the Alexandrian pogrom of 38 CE; the annihilation of 115–117 CE, and the expulsion from Alexandria in 415 CE. Even though these events affected Alexandrian Jews more than other Jews living in Egypt, the centrality of that community was of such importance that there was a knock-on effect for other Jews in the region.

The relationship between Jews and non-Jews in Alexandria was tense. Certainly, there was contact between groups, but sources highlighted aggression from both sides. According to Philo, Alexandrian Jews were massively attacked by pagans in 38 CE: several Jews were killed, synagogues destroyed, and houses burned. The level of violence was, as Erich Gruen (2002, 67) remarks, new. After the pogrom, Jews were allowed to live only in one of the five Alexandrian quarters, probably forming—according to Stroumsa (2012, 258)—the first *ghetto*. But the worst was yet to come. During the Trajan campaign against the Parthians that began in 114 CE, eastern Jewish communities rebelled against the Romans. Egyptian Jews, who had not rebelled in the Jewish War (66–70 CE), joined the movement against Rome. The result of that decision was a retaliation that destroyed the majority of the Jewish communities of Egypt between 115 and 117 CE.[2]

That annihalation can be seen in the epigraphic evidence. Despite the fact that inscriptions found in Egypt were scarce in relation with the estimated Jewish population between antiquity and late antiquity, only thirteen out of 135 were written after the second century (Horbury and Noy 1993).

Despite the notoriety of the Cairo *Genizah*, the manuscripts found there were written from the ninth century onward.[3] Nevertheless, papyri related to Jews uncovered in late ancient Egypt also reveal a decline of the Jewish population after 117 CE. Papyri written by Jews and mentions of Jews in papyri reappeared only in the mid-third century.[4] But, again, after the first third of the fourth century, there are few documents mentioning Jews or written by them.[5] On the other hand, the few papyri found show that Jews held a range of positions in society, namely landowners, farmers, peasants, traders and sailors (Haas, 106–7).

Probably the best-known papyrus is a *Ketubah* (a type of Jewish marriage contract) written in Antinopolis both in Aramaic and Greek, dated to 417 CE (Sirat et al. 1986). It could be associated with the rabbinization process that we saw in Italy and North Africa. Other papyri show a similar development of Hebrew and Aramaic.[6] On the other hand, it is possible that the rabbinization and Hebraization phenomena depended on immigration from Palestine after 117 CE. The *Ketubah* reminds us that Egyptian Jews were not only living in Alexandria.

What can archaeology contribute to this panorama? Unfortunately, almost nothing. Even though there is written evidence of Jewish temples in Elephantine and Heliopolis, and synagogues in several Egyptian cities including Alexandria, no Jewish archaeological remains have ever been found.[7] Some inscriptions containing the word προσευχή, (*Proseuche*, synagogue) were uncovered, but no building has been found.[8]

Last but not least, it is also important to consider (albeit briefly) Egyptian magical texts and artifacts—mainly amulets—both Jewish and Christian, written in the period under study (Bohak 2008). As we will see below, in the section regarding magic bowls of Babylonia, it is not always possible to distinguish between "Jewish" or "Christian" amulets because there was a shared magical culture. In fact, "Jewish" magical texts incorporated foreign elements, while "Christian" amulets also employed non-Christian components, including certain Jewish words. However, Bohak (2008) stressed the particularity of Jewish magic, while Boustan and Sanzo (2017) challenged a simplistic view around shared magical practices. They suggested that certain "Jewish" names and words that appeared in Christian magical texts no longer carried Jewish meanings.

As a preliminary conclusion, sources show a strong and dynamic Jewish life in Egypt from Hellenistic times up to the Jewish Revolt in 115-117 and, after that, a reduced and volatile continuing existence, marked with sporadic attacks, mainly in Alexandria.

The more important sources about Jewish communities during late antiquity, also in Egypt, are Christian. However, they do not provide much information. Origen

(185–254 CE) is a good starting point, but his texts are not free of problems. First of all, even though he was born in Alexandria, he traveled to Rome in 211–212, to Arabia in 213–214, and to the Land of Israel in 215–216. After a conflict with the bishop of Alexandria, he moved to Caesarea in Palestine in 231. He continued to travel, but Caesarea remained his home until his death in 254. These facts are important because it is difficult to obtain information about the period in which Origen lived in Alexandria. Even his texts written in that city could have been edited later in the Land of Israel. Thus, it is not clear if his knowledge about Judaism was produced in an Egyptian or in a Palestinian milieu.

Origen wrote many texts. He used the typical anti-Jewish discourses in his production, attacking Jews for their rejection of Jesus. Nevertheless, he did not write a specific work against them and had frequent contact with Jews, not only for the purposes of debate, but also to improve his knowledge of Hebrew. His writing shows exegetical strategies similar to rabbinical ones. Certainly, Origen's main problem were pagans and certain Gnostics, who were religious groups that denied the validity of the Old Testament. From that point of view, he defended the legitimacy of the Jewish Bible, obviously criticizing Jews for their reaction against Jesus.[9]

But, again, no vital information about Alexandrian Jews can be found.[10] It is necessary to keep in mind that Origen was born seventy years after the Jewish revolt against Trajan. As already stated, only at the end of the third century did Egyptian Jews—according to the papyrological record—become (partially) visible again. There is, however, a text—*De Principiis*—written during this Alexandrian period that reveals some knowledge about rabbinic Judaism. As De Lange (1978, p. 39 ff.) suggested, Origen knew the rabbinical stipulation about the distance that a man can walk during *Sabbath* (two thousand cubits), a measurement written in the *Mishnah*. Were there rabbinized Alexandrian Jews at the beginning of the third century? It was highlighted here that some papyri display signs of Hebraization in the fifth century, but more evidence is needed. In fact, De Lange (1978, 40) suggested that it is difficult to know if Origen reedited *De Principiis* in the Land of Israel or if he acquired the rabbinical information during his first travel to Palestine. On the other hand, in his *Contra Celsum,* Origen demonstrates—through the pagan Celsus—that he was familiar with Jewish narratives against Jesus, similar to *Toledot Yeshu* traditions.[11] Thus, Origen exhibited theological anti-Judaism and, at the same time, contact with the Jewish community. The problem is that his own life makes it difficult to know which Jews he had contact with and where.

We have mentioned the expulsion of the Alexandrian community accomplished by the bishop Cyril (ca. 370–444 CE) in 414–415. Christopher Haas (1997, 122) suggested that that situation was an exception and it should not be extrapolated to the whole period. However, although it is true that interaction was the rule, it is also true that there were intense tensions between Jews and Christians, and the events of 414–415 were a watershed.

Cyril's rhetoric was fiercely anti-Jewish, even before becoming bishop of Alexandria. Haas correctly stated that after the destruction of the pagan *Serapeum* in 391 CE, Jews became the most significant religious adversary. Even though there is no evidence of Judaizing attitudes in Alexandria, Cyril considered the existence of a significant alternative religious community to be intolerable. The opportunity came, according to *Socrates Scholasticus,* from a Jewish attack. After a conflict between Jews and Christians related to Jewish attendance to the theatre on Saturdays, one night Jews spread the notice that the main

Alexandrian church was on fire. When Christians arrived at the place, Jews killed a great number of them in the ambush. The following day Cyril gathered a big crowd, seized all the synagogues—converting some of them to churches, burning others—and evicted the Jews, while also destroying houses and shops. It is difficult to pin down precisely what happened, but it is important to highlight that the Jewish population was not passive and often reacted violently against Christians and pagans (Irshai 2013). On the other hand, there is a debate around the continuing survival of the Jewish settlement in Alexandria (Stroumsa 2012; Irshai 2013). Even accepting its continuity, the Jewish population of the city was certainly reduced. It is more difficult to trace the situation of other Jewish Egyptian communities, but epigraphic and papyrological records also show a decline.

Leontius of Neapolis said, in the seventh century, that there were Jews living in Alexandria.[12] The *Genizah* found in Cairo revealed that, up to the ninth century, the vitality of Egyptian Jews was reborn. Whether this was the result of fresh immigration—as was probably the case after 117 CE—or indigenous growth, it is difficult to answer.

Notes

[1] Currently, the *Septuagint* is seen as the conclusion of a long process of translation that involved different places of the Diaspora and even the Land of Israel. On the *Septuagint* see Rajak 2009.

[2] On the destruction of Jewry in 115-117 CE, see Kerkeslager 2006. In contrast, stating continuity based on papyrological evidence (outside Alexandria) and a supposedly Jewish Alexandrian embassy to Rome, Haas 1997, 103-9.

[3] Some manuscripts are probably copies of previous texts. However, up to this day scholars have not found any significant information about late ancient Egyptian Jews there.

[4] See Tcherikover 1957, 94 (= I CPJ). Papyri related to late ancient Egypt were compiled in Tcherikover et al. 1964 (= III CPJ).

For Jewish literary works written in papyrus, see van Haelst 1976, who also sees a decline in the second century. *Ostraca* are also important to reconstruct Jewish life.

[5] Tal Ilan (2016), who is compiling an update of CPJ, criticizes Tcherikover's compilation, mainly for ignoring papyri in Aramaic and Hebrew. She thinks that the new found papyri and new criteria of compilation, shows continuity of the Jewish settlement after 117 CE. In addition, she believes that Egyptian Jewish communities between the fifth and seventh centuries were more important than Tcherikover affirmed. However, even with the new manuscripts, the panorama outlined by Tcherikover has not changed dramatically. Nevertheless, it is necessary to await Ilan's publication of IV CPJ before drawing definite conclusions.

[6] Haas (1997, 122 ff.) believed that processes of Hebraization and rabbinization became pronounced in the last part of the fourth century. Nevertheless more evidence is necessary to support the idea of an early Hebraization. Also Ilan (2016) observes the increasing use of Aramaic and Hebrew in Egypt after the fourth century, although she sustains that both languages were important even before that. She also highlights the importance of papyri with *piyyutim* that demonstrate a strong link between Egypt and the Land of Israel.

[7] The only exception could be the ancient temple of Elephantine, where certain authors (see Rosenberg 2004) suggested that a floor of better quality uncovered in the "Aramaic quarter" was a temple of Yahweh dating from the fifth century BCE, referred to in papyri of that period. However, it is difficult to confirm if the excavated structure belonged to the mentioned temple.

[8] Levine (2005, 21 ff.) recognized that Egyptian inscriptions of the third century BCE were the first "hard" evidence of synagogues, but he opted for Palestine as the place where synagogues originated.

[9] On Origen and the Jews, see De Lange 1978 and Drake 2013, 38–58.

[10] There are mentions of Judaism in Clement of Alexandria as well. Nevertheless, he referred mainly to *rhetorical Jews*. On Clement and the Jews, see Carleton Paget 1998. See also *Timothy and Aquila*, a polemical text written between the fifth and sixth century, probably in Egypt.

[11] On the statements against Christians expressed by the figure of the Jew in the *Contra Celsum* as a reproduction of real Jewish-Alexandrian anti-Christian arguments, see Niehoff 2013.

[12] See Haas 1997, 127, and Stroumsa 2012. There are also references—though imprecise—in John of Nikiu and Michael the Syrian. On the other hand, according to Anastasius Sinaita there was a Jewish philosopher called Acoluthos in sixth-century Alexandria.

Chapter 7

The Land of Israel

It is impossible to summarize the history of the Jews in the Land of Israel during late antiquity in a few pages, but we can present an overview. However, first it is necessary to lay out the most important events of the period.

After the defeat of the Jewish Revolt (66–70 CE), Jewish communities began a slow reorganization. In 132 CE, Jews—under the leadership of Bar Kokhba—rebelled once more against Rome. Again they were defeated and that event represented a hard blow for Jewish communities in Palestine. Gradually, the centre of Jewish life moved from Judea to Galilee (Levine 1992; Sivan 2008, 317–28). Meanwhile, Christianity grew slowly in Palestine. This is not the place to discuss the precise moment of the "parting of the ways" but in the first two centuries CE, differences between Jews and Christians were not as obvious as they are for a modern observer. Here it is worth mentioning Israel Yuval's (2006) polemical position: Rabbinical Judaism as a response to Christianity. Even though Yuval's point of view was not accepted by all scholars, his works are important as they remind us that rabbinical Judaism was a new creation. As Alan Segal (1986) has previously stated, both religions, rabbinical Judaism and Christianity, were not father and son, but brothers.

Unlike other regions we have studied, there are several late ancient texts written by Jews in Palestine that have survived to the present day. The *Mishnah* was written at the beginning of the third century and compiles a series of laws regarding different areas of Jewish life, such as agriculture, criminal law, marriage, idolatry, etc. *Tosefta* is another collection, similar to the *Mishnah*, also edited in the Land of Israel around the same time. Finally, the *Talmud Yerushalmi*—completed around the fourth to fifth centuries—commented on certain mishnaic tractates. *Genesis Rabbah*, *Leviticus Rabbah*, and *Pesikta de-Rav Kahana,* among others, were also produced in the period.[1]

All this written production offers a significant amount of information, which represents a big advantage over other regions we have seen in previous chapters. Nevertheless, as stated in the introduction, rabbinical texts are not straightforward. In fact, the *Yerushalmi* compiled different rabbinical *dicta* attributed to rabbis between the second century BCE and fourth century CE. As we will also see in the *Bavli*, there is a long-running debate around changes— or additions—made by the final editors of the texts (if we accept the existence of final editors).

While rabbis were compiling—or creating—the *Yesushalmi*, an important change happened in the Roman Empire: Constantine legalized Christianity and developed a pro-Christian policy. In spite of the fact that he only converted himself to Christianity on his deathbed, and that only after Theodosius I did the empire become officially Christian, Constantine's decision had a direct impact on Palestine's topography. Indeed, the proliferation of churches such as the Holy Sepulchre changed the shape of Jerusalem and accelerated the movement of Jews to Galilee. Indeed, after the fourth century, Jerusalem gradually became a Christian city. It is necessary to stress that the process was progressive because up to the fourth century the Christian population in the Land of Israel was sparse.

But gradually the Christianization of the empire became central. Concerning legislation, the situation of the Jews deteriorated. As we have seen, the *Codex Theodosianus* marginalized Jews. But the *Justinian Code*—promulgated in 529 and 534 and widely used in the east—was even tougher (Rabello 2006; Tolan et al. 2014). Two of Justinian's well-known *novellae* are good examples. As noted in Chapter 3, *novella 37* established the conversion of every African synagogue into a church in 535 CE. In addition, in the *Novella 146* Περί Εβραίων—enacted in 553 CE—Justinian determined that Greek, Latin, or any other language was allowed to be employed during the Jewish liturgy. According to him, the decree arose from an internal dispute among Jews regarding the use of Hebrew or Greek in the synagogues. He also stated that, when reading the Bible in Greek, the *Septuagint* or Akilas' translation had to be used. Although there are disagreements around the language that was used previously by the Jews, the majority of scholars believe that the *novella* confirmed the Hebraization process and its tensions.[2] Furthermore, the law shows the interference of the Christian emperor in Jewish internal issues.

Less than a century later and after the ephemeral Persian conquest of Jerusalem in 614 CE—probably with Jewish help[3]—Emperor Heraclius decreed the forced conversion of Jews of the empire. Certainly, it is not clear if the measure was implemented or not. Neither is it possible to know—if indeed it was applied—the extent of forced conversions (Dagron and Déroche 2010, 17–46).

Beyond these macro political events, what do we know about Jewish life in the Land of Israel? As stated previously, there are many sources that reconstruct that history and hundreds of pages would be necessary to deal with them in full.[4] Let us summarize the available sources, beginning with the archaeological and epigraphic record.

As Seth Schwartz (2001) stated, cities of the Land of Israel during late antiquity looked like typical Roman cities. Even in the most important Jewish settlement—Galilee—it is very difficult to find specific Jewish features apart from synagogues. In cities like Sepphoris or Tiberias, there were Roman baths, theatres, temples, and pagan imagery (Dauphin 1998). Indeed, the rabbinical movement left few archaeological traces in Palestine during the first four centuries CE. According to Schwartz, Judaism practically disappeared in the region, except for the marginal rabbinical group. But even rabbis needed to coexist with the pagan environment, as the anecdote of Rabbi Gamaliel in a Roman bath with an Aphrodite sculpture, narrated in the *Mishnah*, shows.[5]

Certainly, Schwartz's thesis is quite radical. According to him, Jews were using pagan imagery not as mere ornamentation. Furthermore, he believed there were Jews who "forgot" their Judaism. However, there are more moderate historiographical positions. For example, Hayim Lapin (2012) suggests that the rabbinical group was a new movement, a product of the provincialization and Romanization of the Jewish elite. This sub-elite was the result of negotiation between the Jewish past and the Roman domination. Lapin also states that the rabbinical movement was marginal until the fourth century. It was marginal even within the sparse Jewish population, which did not forget Judaism but instead had different conceptions of it.

As mentioned above, there is one distinctive Jewish building in the region: the synagogue. The large majority of late ancient synagogues were found in Galilee and they date from between the fourth and eighth centuries

CE. There were also synagogues in central and southern Palestine, but they were fewer than in Galilee (Werlin 2015). Thus, archaeological evidence confirms that Galilee was the most important Jewish settlement in late antiquity.

A controversy seethes around the rabbinical—or non-rabbinical—character of late ancient synagogues. According to certain authors such as Zeev Safrai (1995), synagogues were strongly associated with the rabbinical movement. However, the majority of scholars have highlighted that there is no significant evidence to affirm that. First, only a few rabbis are mentioned in the epigraphic material found in synagogues. Second, certain architectural and iconographical features do not correspond with traditions found in the rabbinic literature. Indeed, the iconography uncovered in several synagogues contributed to increasing the complexity of the definition. Zodiacs were discovered in the pavement of the synagogues of Sepphoris, Beit Alpha and Hammat Tiberias, among others. It is important to highlight that Hammat Tiberias and Beit Alpha also have representations of Helios in the centre of the zodiacal disk.[6] Beyond the discussion about its meaning—a simple calendar, an ornament, a religious manifestation, etc.—rabbinic literature was generally against that kind of art. Furthermore, human representations were found in synagogue pavements and reliefs. To give an example, the beautiful synagogue of Huqoq—uncovered in 2011—not only contains images of elephants but also representations of humans: a general (possibly Alexander the Great) and his soldiers. In Beit Alpha, human representations included biblical scenes such as the Binding of Isaac. Were these synagogues decorated against rabbinical will? Or were they approved by the rabbis? The answer is problematic, because although strict rabbinic literature rejected figural art, some fragments of the *Talmudim* are ambiguous. As

Catherine Hezser (2010, 22-23) suggests, it is important to avoid the historiographical practice that strictly separates rabbis from non-rabbis. There were synagogues that were probably built by non-rabbinical groups, but others could have been built—or accepted—by the rabbinical movement. Interaction between rabbinical and non-rabbinical Jews was common. On the other hand, there were also differences within the rabbinical movement itself. Moreover, as stated above, the rabbinical movement was marginal until the fourth century and did not achieve complete control of Judaism until the sixth century.

Late ancient Jewish art changed dramatically around the seventh to eighth centuries. In fact, synagogues such as Na'aran or Susiya were modified by iconoclasts. Human—and sometimes animal—figures were destroyed and occasionally replaced by geometric designs. New synagogues, as in Jericho, were built without figural art. Only the specific Jewish repertoire was kept: the *menorah*, *etrog*, *shofar*, Torah shrine, etc. Those iconoclastic interventions have been read in different ways. Some scholars see a replication of the wider iconoclastic movement in Christendom, others, the influence of Islam, and certain researchers consider that iconoclasm represented the final victory of the (naturally) iconoclastic rabbinical movement.[7] Again, no consensus has been reached but the fact is that the beautiful and complex synagogal Jewish art from late antiquity disappeared after the eighth century. Finally, it is necessary to highlight, as Steven Fine (2010) did when he analyzed art in the Jewish catacombs of the Land of Israel, that "Jewish art" in late antiquity was similar to Graeco-Roman art. In fact, "Jewish art" could be considered a branch of Graeco-Roman art.

Architectural features of the synagogue are useful in reconstructing some important issues of daily religious life. For example, the growing area allotted to the Torah in late ancient Palestinian synagogues revealed the centrality of reading the Pentateuch. The same phenomenon can be seen in relation to synagogal pavements representing biblical scenes, or even Torah arks. On the other hand, the existence of guest chambers and different rooms remind us of the importance of the synagogue as a communal centre.[8]

Other characteristics are important too. Most of the synagogues in the Land of Israel were oriented toward Jerusalem, implying that even though Galilee was the new Judaic centre, Jerusalem kept its central place in the Jewish worldview. As we saw when studying iconography, the shape of synagogues was also influenced by their environment. Thus, synagogues uncovered in the Golan Heights had structures similar to non-Jewish buildings in Syria. Despite attempts to establish architectural synagogal types in the Land of Israel, diversity was the rule. Even in a single region, for example Beit She'an, Levine (2005, p. 215 ff.) demonstrated the variability of architectural patterns of five contemporary synagogues.[9]

It is necessary to highlight that despite Theodosian and Justinian codes prohibiting the erection or reformation of Jewish temples, synagogues continued to be built and refurbished in the Land of Israel during the whole period of late antiquity. Not less important, archaeological studies have demonstrated that no dramatic demographic decline occurred in the Land of Israel during late antiquity. In fact, except for Judea, the Jewish population remained stable or even increased in the rest of Palestine, principally Galilee and the Golan. The quantity of written production from the period confirms the vitality of Jewish communities in the region.

The other specific Jewish archaeological remains are cemeteries and catacombs. From these remains, a great amount of information can be obtained. In this sense, the most important late ancient site related to Judaism in the Land of Israel is Beit She'arim, in Lower Galilee (Kraemer 2001). It is the major Jewish necropolis—composed of more than twenty-five catacombs dating from between the third and fifth century CE—in which Jews of Israel and from different places of the Diaspora were buried. However, as Fine suggests (2010, 455), the catacombs of Beit She'arim had scant Jewish identity markers. In fact, beside a small repertoire of icons and certain inscriptions, the architecture and iconography are similar to pagan and Christian ones. Even rabbis were buried in catacombs with pagan symbolism.

As in the synagogues, the specific Jewish iconographic repertoire consisted of *menorah*, *shofar*, *lulav*, *etrog*, etc. Along with these symbols are found a neutral set of motifs, usually used by pagans: doors, ships, horses, lions, skeletons, and masks, among others. Furthermore, there are also human figures. Even images representing gods, like the goddess Victoria, are found in the catacombs. Again, this kind of iconography shows that rabbinical measures were not taken by all the Jews. It does not necessarily imply that rabbis did not use the catacombs, but it shows once again that the rabbinical movement was slowly growing, and Judaism was a multifaceted phenomenon. This can also demonstrate that even inside the rabbinical movement there were different perspectives regarding art.

One of the catacombs is particularly eminent because Judah the Prince (*Yehuda Ha-Nasi*), the redactor—according to the tradition—of the *Mishnah* was allegedly buried there. In fact, catacomb 14 is not only a monumental site, inscriptions with the names of the sons of Judah were found *in situ*.[10] This brings us to the discussion about epigraphic rabbis. In 1981 Shaye Cohen stated that not only is the

word "rabbi" scarcely present in late ancient Jewish epigraphy—throughout the Mediterranean—but also that the few
mentions found implied an honorific title not directly linked
to the rabbinical movement.[11] Even though Cohen's perspective gained consensus in its time, later on different scholars
questioned his statements and currently most researchers
consider that certain epigraphic rabbis were undoubtedly
linked to the rabbinical movement (Hezser 2010, 25).

Regarding epigraphy, different types of information can be obtained.[12] The languages used by Jews is an
important issue. In general, "rabbis" epitaphs were written
in Aramaic or Hebrew, yet most Palestinian late ancient
inscriptions are in Greek. In fact, only in Judea, the Golan
and certain villages of Galilee, do Hebrew and Aramaic
inscriptions reach the same number as Greek ones (Smelik
2010, 128). Altogether, between 60 and 70 per cent of
Jewish late ancient epigraphy uncovered in the Land of
Israel was written in Greek (Smelik 2010, 135). Even inside
synagogues, Greek is significant, representing a third of
the inscriptions (Fine 2010). However, it is important to
highlight a diachronic and regional feature: a Hebraization
process can be seen slowly from the second century
onward, mainly in the countryside.

On the other hand, the epigraphic record also shows—
after the fourth century—the gradual rabbinization of the
population. The presence of talmudic references confirms
the slow but definite growth of rabbinical culture in the
Land of Israel. Nevertheless, we must bear in mind that
just a small proportion of the Jews—those who had mid and
high economic status—had epigraphic habits and, because
of that, generalizations should be made with caution.

Before analyzing rabbinic literature, it is important
to draw attention to another kind of text that survived
from the period. Even before late antiquity, the letters of
Babatha's family found in the Judaean desert dating from

the Bar Kokhba period, are useful. These papyri confirmed the multiplicity of languages employed in the region, at least in wealthy circles. They were written mainly in Greek, but also in Aramaic and Nabatean. Among the letters, a marriage contract that is very different to the *Ketubah* imposed by rabbis was found. This shows, again, the diversity within Judaism.[13]

Now it is time to address the rabbinic literature. As mentioned previously, the material produced by rabbis during late antiquity is by far the most important written production of the period. However, it is necessary to understand that those texts were written with a performative purpose. Thus, texts do not only display ideas, worldviews and certain realities, but also the society that rabbis desired. This means that rabbinical sources should be interpreted very carefully because it is not easy to separate wishes, projections, and realities. They exaggerated their influence, not only in their own time but also in earlier centuries. Because of that, archaeological and epigraphic evidence should be studied alongside rabbinical texts, not to confirm facts but to compare them and enrich the panorama (Meyer 2014).

What does rabbinic literature say about Jews in late antiquity? Rabbis spoke more about rabbis and norms than about non-rabbis (Jews or non-Jews). References to the common Jewish population—generally called *am ha'aretz*—are scarce and always negative. Therefore, we should begin with the rabbinical group. It was stated previously that its growth was gradual. In fact, rabbis during the second century should be seen as a minority faction. Even though the *Yerushalmi* attempted to exaggerate rabbinical power, certain passages of the text demonstrate that rabbinical authority was questioned by several Jews (Hezser 1997, 386–402).

In their beginnings, rabbis were just a wealthy elite whose decisions were only voluntarily adopted by other

Jews. The first rabbis—the *Tannaim*—were prosperous men, generally landowners who usually distinguished themselves from poor people. The next generations—rabbis known as *Amoraim*—were more heterogeneous, but most of them held a comfortable economic position (Lapin 2012). It is important to keep in mind that this was an agricultural society and rabbis were directly or indirectly linked to farming activities.

Sometimes they lived in big cities, and, as we said previously, late ancient cities in the Land of Israel were pagan and, later, Christian. All in all, as Joshua Schwartz (2006, 452) states, the material reality of Jewish life in Palestine during late antiquity was not very different from the non-Jewish one. Of course, religious practices were diverse, but the daily life of a Jew, a pagan, or a Christian was quite similar.

Rabbis were aware of language diversity in the Land of Israel. Even though they promoted Hebrew and Aramaic, they accepted other languages for certain situations, for example in *y* (= *Yerushalmi, Jerusalem Talmud*) *Sotah* 21b–21c. They also attempted to impose their ideas about food permitted for consumption (Rosenblum 2010). They sought to control the judicial system as well, using private courts that only issued judgments when both parties voluntarily agreed to rabbinical participation.

But Jewish communities in Palestine were not alone. The rabbis knew that and struggled to control the interaction among religious groups. In fact, *Avoda Zara*—*Mishnah*'s tractate and *Yerushalmi*'s commentary—were entirely dedicated to regulating contact between Jews and non-Jews. The main target of Palestinian rabbis was not Christianity—which was not very strong until the fourth century—but pagan religiosity. Thus, *Avoda Zara* stipulated ordinances related to pagan habits and celebrations such as the Calends.[14] Contacts with non-Jews were not forbidden—it was impossible to avoid in pagan cities—but regulated. For example, Jews were not allowed to trade with pagans before and after their festivals and rituals in *m* (= *Mishnah*) *Avoda Zara* 1, 3, and in *y Avoda Zara* 39a ff.

The remarkable scarcity of references to Christianity in early Palestinian rabbinic literature has generated much debate. This issue is impossible to tackle in a few pages, but from our point of view that absence was the result of the slow growth of Christianity in the Land of Israel at the time of the *Mishnah* and, even the *Yerushalmi*.[15] However, Christians living in Palestine did speak about Jews. Jerome (ca. 340–420 CE), who interacted with Jews during his time in the Land of Israel, is a good example (Stemberger 1993). In fact, he had Jewish teachers who helped him learn Hebrew. He also said that Jews continued to go to the ruins of the Second Temple on the Ninth of Av in order to mourn (*In Sophoniam* 1.15). Furthermore, he referred to the Jewish δευτερώσεις, a probable translation of תנא (*tana*) that could indicate that he had met rabbis.[16] He also described the Land of Israel as a place overrun by Jews, Samaritans, and Pagans, but we must remember that Christian literature often overstates the size of the adversary.[17] All in all, Christian authors such as Jerome exhibit interaction between communities. Interactions that rabbis decided not to record, probably because they did not consider it important or urgent.

Christian sources are also important in reconstructing political facts that Jews did not state in their texts. For example, the majority of the testimonies on the Jewish rebellion against Constantius Gallus in 351–352 CE derived from Christian sources: Chrysostom, Jerome, Socrates of Constantinople, and Sozomen.[18] Even though the rebellion was not very important, it represents the most significant Jewish military action after the Bar Kokhba revolt.[19] Again, the problem with Christian sources is that they are often polemical and generic.

Pagan sources also provide information about Jews. The rebellion of Constantius Gallus was recorded by Aurelius Victor (*Liber de Caesaribus* 42, 11). On the other hand, Libanius, to give another example, wrote letters to the Jewish Patriarch.[20] These letters show a cordial relationship between the two men, in contrast with certain aggressive references found in Libanius' other texts.

This brings us to the figure of the Jewish Patriarch. It is not easy to measure the real power of this office during late antiquity. Different laws in the *Theodosian Code* attributed him juridical prerogatives within the Jewish community, and referred to him using honorific titles such as *clarissimus*. The office remained active until the first third of the fifth century. Furthermore, one question remains open and concerns the extent of the Patriarch's jurisdiction in the Jewish community. As Goodblat (2006) explains, some scholars see the Patriarch as just a member of a stronger rabbinical dynasty, while others consider he held a different kind of power. From our point of view, the relationship with the Roman Empire gave special influence to the Patriarch, even though his power should not be overstated. He was an important interlocutor for the empire and he certainly had influence—though not without tensions—in rabbinical circles.

Finally, where were the non-rabbinical Jews? This is a difficult question to answer because rabbis said little about non-rabbis. As we have already remarked, certain texts reveal tensions with the rabbinical way of life, and rabbis always despised the *am ha'aretz*. Thus, the voice of non-rabbinical—or not entirely rabbinical—Jews did not survive.[21] Undeniably, the archaeological and epigraphic record could help us to imagine a multifaceted Judaism, but our available insights into the worldview of non-rabbinical Jews is very limited. All in all, it is important to highlight that in all likelihood rabbinical and non-rabbinical Jews were not so very different. Indeed, Jews, Christians, and pagans in the Land of Israel were more similar than popular representations suggest.

Notes

[1] For a brief introduction to Palestinian rabbinical texts, see Strack and Stemberger 1996.

[2] On the *Novella 146*, see Colorni 1964 and Rutgers 2009, among others.

[3] On the Persian conquest of Jerusalem, see Avi-Yonah 1978, 257–72 and Sivan 2000.

[4] For an excellent summary and analysis on sources to reconstruct Jewish history in the Land of Israel during late antiquity, see Hezser 2010.

[5] M (= *Mishnah*) Avoda *Zara* 3, 4. On the discussion between Gamaliel and a pagan philosopher in a Roman bath in Acco, see Friedheim 2006, 92–107.

[6] On Jewish, Pagan, Christian, and Muslim pavements in late ancient Palestine, see Talgam 2014. Specifically related to synagogal pavements in the period, Fine 2005, and Hachlili 2013.

[7] On iconoclasm in Jewish synagogues, see Yuval-Hacham 2010.

[8] The Theodotus inscription—found in Jerusalem and dating from the first century CE—stated that the synagogue had been built "for the reading of the Torah and for teaching of the commandments, and the guest rooms, the chambers and water fittings for the need of strangers...". The inscription not only shows the importance of the reading of the Torah—even in an earlier period—but also the communal significance of the building. The original Greek text and the translation in Hachlili 2013, 524.

[9] On late ancient Palestinian synagogues in general, see also Ribak 2007, Hachlili 2013, and Fine 2014. The analysis of *Batei Midrash* (houses of study), whose archaeological remains can be easily confused with synagogues or are never discovered at all due to their simplicity, is very difficult.

[10] See Kraemer 2001, 63–65. According to *b Ketubot* 103a-b, Judah the Prince was buried in Beit She'arim.

[11] On the debate around epigraphic rabbis, see also Lapin 2011, among others.

[12] Ancient Jewish inscriptions from Palestine were compiled by Frey (1952). An updated compilation in Cotton et al. 2010–2012

(inscriptions from Jerusalem), Ameling et al. 2011 (Caesarea and the middle coast), and 2014 (south coast). This collection will be completed with the publication of volumes on the Negev and Galilee respectively.

[13] On the Babatha archive, see Smelik 2010. After this archive, there is a hiatus of almost four hundred years until the next discovered Jewish papyrus in the region. See Cotton 2013.

[14] See for example, m *Avoda Zara* 1, 3, and y *Avoda Zara* 39c. On the identification of Pagan festivals in the *Talmud*, see Friedheim 2006.

[15] There are no more than five direct references to Jesus in *Tosefta* and *Yerushalmi*. See, on this topic, Schäfer 2007 and Murcia 2014. On the other hand, Yuval (2006) suggested that mentions of Christianity were deliberately omitted in order to overturn that religion. Indeed, Yuval thinks that the rabbinic literature was an answer to the New Testament. Also emphasizing the importance of Christianity and its influence in the growth of the rabbinical movement, see Boyarin 1999 and 2004. From our point of view, rabbis knew of Christianity but they were not obsessed with it.

[16] Jerome, *Epistulae,* 121, 10. On the use of δευτερώσεις instead of אנה, see Stemberger 1993, 354. It is important to highlight that this fragment does not mechanically mean that Jerome had contact with rabbis.

[17] Jerome, *Epistulae*, 93. See Sivan 2008, 166. Again, we should approach Jerome's information carefully.

[18] For a complete list of Christian authors that wrote about the Jewish revolt against Constantius, see Stern 1980, 501. On the rebellion, see Stemberger 1999, 161–84.

[19] The revolt was tangentially referred to in rabbinical sources, but without mentioning Constantius or providing information about the event. For a list of rabbinical references, see Stern 1980, 501.

[20] On Libanius's epistles to the Jewish Patriarch, see Stern 1980, 589–97. A minority group of scholars think that Libanius's communications were sent to the Christian Patriarch.

[21] It is important to mention again the position of Philip Alexander (2010), who reminds us that certain texts which we call rabbinical, were written, perhaps, by different (and even non-rabbinical) groups. However, it is really hard to develop a picture of them. See n. 9 (Chapter 1).

Chapter 8

Babylonia

In *b Kiddushin* 69b, a Palestinian rabbi stated that Jewish Babylonian genealogy, thanks to a decision of Ezra, was purer than the Palestinian one. This declaration reflects the conviction of Babylonian rabbis (by means of the *Bavli*) about the shift of the rabbinical centre from the Land of Israel to Mesopotamia, a territory under control of the Sassanid Empire and called Babylonia by the Jews.

Even though the *Bavli* is also a commentary on the *Mishnah*, it differs from the *Yerushalmi* in various aspects. First of all, it was finished later, between the sixth and seventh centuries. This question is not as uncomplicated as it may seem because, as we have seen, there are numerous disagreements about the final redaction of the text. It is presented as a compilation of rabbinical interpretations from the second century BCE up to the fifth century CE. There are also anonymous statements, the dating of which is still debated. On the other hand, the *Bavli* has a different style to the *Yerushalmi*. It is less centred on legal issues and it dedicates more space to stories. Moreover, in contrast to the *Yerushalmi*, only *Berakhot*, out of the eleven agricultural mishnaic tractates, was commented on in the *Bavli*.[1]

Before tackling rabbinic literature, we will first discuss archaeological remains. Unfortunately, no important

Jewish ruins were found in Babylonia. No synagogue or academy has been discovered in the most important rabbinical land. No Jewish cemeteries or graves have been uncovered in the region.[2] Only two types of artifacts have been found: seals and magic bowls.

Let's begin with seals. They were used in the Sassanid Empire by kings, *magi* (Zoroastrian priests), officers, merchants, and the wealthy in general. They were small pieces, with a name and an emblem. Less than fifty Sassanid Jewish seals have been identified.[3] Indeed, identification of Jewish seals is not straightforward, as most of the motifs used by Jews were also used by Zoroastrians and Christians. Additionally, all the seals we have were obtained on the black market and as a result, there can be no certitude about the sites of provenance. Only the seals that contain Hebrew, Aramaic, or specific Jewish iconography have been decisively identified as Jewish. This means that several seals, probably used by Jews, cannot be recognized as such, which leads us to believe that Babylonian Jews used more Jewish identity markers than they actually employed. On top of this, it is difficult to date the seals.

But beyond these difficulties, certain conclusions can be reached. Some of the seals identify rabbis mentioned in the *Bavli*. The most important is Huna bar Nathan (Friedenberg 2009, n. 9), *amora*, and Exilarch from the fourth century. Even though the identification is not absolutely certain, most scholars agree with it. Thus, the seals provide physical proof of the existence of rabbis in the region.

Seals also give us a glimpse of Jewish iconography—or art—in Babylonia. They exhibit very few specific motifs related to Jews. Indeed, only the combination of *etrog* and *lulav* can be described as specifically Jewish. This is important because representations of these *Sukkot* fruits were found in almost every region inhabited by Jews in late antiquity. On the other hand, the absence of *menorah* designs is remarkable. Perhaps seals with *menoroth* remain to be found, or Sassanid Jews did not use the image, unlike the entire Jewish iconography of the Diaspora and the Land of Israel.[4] Along with the *etrog* and the *lulav*, there are illustrations used also by Christians and Zoroastrians: lions, rams, bears, pheasants, roosters, stars, the Moon, etc. Figural portrayals are not absent: there are Jewish seals in which the Binding of Isaac is represented. Despite most of the seals with that design being Christian (they have crosses), two seals have Hebrew letters and no crosses. The motifs were also used in certain synagogal mosaic pavements in Palestine, as in Beit Alpha, Susiya, and Sepphoris. Other seals have no crosses or Hebrew inscription and can be interpreted as being either Jewish or Christian.

Seals with the representation of Daniel inside the Lion's den were also found. According to Friedenberg (2009, 23–25), they are all Christian. Indeed, there are seals of Daniel with crosses. However, certain pieces only show Daniel with two lions (Fridenberg 2009, nn. 52–55) without crosses, and can be identified as Jewish. It is true that Daniel in an *orans* position (elbows close to the sides of the body and the hands outstretched sideways, palms up) is a Christian motif. However, some Palestine synagogal mosaic pavements—Na'aran and Susiya for example—had the same design. Furthermore, there is a relief in the Ein-Samsan synagogue of Daniel in a clear *orans* position (Fine 2014, 219). On the other hand, three Jewish seals (Friedenberg 2009, nn. 27–29)—reliably identified as such since they were written in Hebrew—contain human figures. Again, these representations show us that Jews used figurative art, even at the heart of the rabbinical land.

Incantation bowls are more intricate than seals because they have longer texts. They date from between the fifth and eighth centuries and were written in Jewish Babylonian Aramaic, also using words from Mandaic and Syriac.[5] The texts they contain are composed principally of magic spells: protection against demons, personal enemies, and curses; protection for babies and the unborn; curses against foes; healing incantations; etc. Most of the bowls were acquired on the black market but a few were uncovered in archaeological excavations, where they were discovered buried upside down. It is important to highlight, as Dan Levene has done (2003, 3), that incantations were not written to be read.

It is equally as important to emphasize that incantation bowls were not exclusively Jewish. Indeed, certain researchers suggested that it is not useful to label magic bowls as "Jewish," "Christian," or "Manichean." Magical practices often reflect knowledge and habits shared by the whole population, without religious distinctions, and incantation bowls are no exception. In fact, certain bowls were translated into the dialect of other religious communities, with no significant changes to the text (Levene 2003, p. 28 ff). On the other hand, in the few official excavations where incantation bowls were uncovered, bowls written in different dialects (Mandaic and Jewish Babylonian Aramaic, for example) were found in the same house. Moreover, certain "Jewish" bowls contained the names of pagan gods and *formulae*. Even Jesus is mentioned on some "Jewish" bowls written in Aramaic (Harviainen 1981; Levene 2003, 120–38). Finally, the names of the owners of "Jewish" incantation bowls are sometimes Zoroastrian, implying it was not only Jews that used these bowls.[6] Because of these facts, Juusola (1999, 84) asserts that incantation bowls were inter-confessional material.

Why, then, do scholars speak about "Jewish" incantation bowls? First, as stressed above, the language.[7] Second, there are quotations from the Old Testament, mainly from liturgical texts. There are invocations also, to Yahweh, and angels (and archangels) such as Gabriel, Michael, Ariel, Raphael, Metatron, etc. In addition, certain bowls contain references similar to *Hekhalot* literature.[8]

Another issue concerns the relationship between rabbis and magic bowls. Scholarship is divided on this point. Some scholars claim that incantations were written by semi-literate sorcerers, while others consider that the same scribes who wrote rabbinical texts inscribed incantation bowls (Levene 2003, 4–7). There are arguments in favour of each position. First, the Aramaic found on magic bowls is similar to Talmudic Aramaic, but not identical (Shaked 2015, 97–98). Thus, it could be the result of scribes who were not rabbinical or just a decision to create a different kind of text. Second, there are rabbis mentioned on incantation bowls. Again, we have the debate around the question: were they "rabbis" as we see in the *Bavli*, or it was just an honorific title?[9] Furthermore, *m Sanhedrin* 10:1 prohibits the use of biblical verses for magic purposes. Why, then, would a rabbi have commissioned a magic bowl? As stated previously, *Talmudim* were intended to shape society. But even members of the rabbinical group exhibited behaviours contradicting what the *Bavli* established. Magic, perhaps, was one of the "deviations" that certain rabbis accepted, without breaking with the rabbinical movement. The conclusion, again, is that practices performed by rabbis were not very different from non-rabbinical (and non-Jewish) groups.

Magic bowls were also illustrated. And, as we saw in the Palestinian synagogues and Jewish Babylonian seals, figurative art is found there. In the case of the bowls, there are portrayals of demons, animals, humans, and hybrid creatures. The type of iconography is similar to the Persian, showing again the influence of the milieu. In fact, the kinds of representations found on the Jewish bowls are very similar to images found on Persian amulets (Vilozny 2013).

Regarding other evidence, there are no Zoroastrian sources from the Talmudic period that mention Judaism.[10] However, Christian texts written in the Sassanid context reveal interaction and tension with the Jews. Aphrahat (ca. 280–ca. 345 CE) and Narsai (ca. 399–ca. 502) are good examples. Certain *Demonstrationes* written by Aphrahat were directed against Jews. In *Demonstratio* 18, for example, he attacked the Jewish attitude towards sex and reproduction.[11] Narsai, in the Persian Nisibis, also vilified the Jews through written texts. It is possible that, as certain scholars have suggested, Aphrahat and Narsai merely repeated pre-existing anti-Jewish clichés. Additionally, as we saw, the term "Jew" was also used as a hermeneutical device in conflicts between different Christian groups. However, even accepting that some texts were not directed against *historical Jews*, evidence taken as a whole seems to confirm that Christians in the Sassanid Empire were interacting with them. As we stated previously, it is difficult to know which kind of Jews—rabbinical or non-rabbinical—they were engaging in dialogue with.

For all of these reasons, rabbinic literature should be taken into consideration. But which period does the *Bavli* reflect? In other words, did the last editors create their own tales and modify stories attributed to previous rabbis? As we said before, there is a controversy around the edition of the *Bavli*. Kalmin (1994) believed that the transmission of earlier traditions was relatively accurate, while others, such as Neusner (1987, among other publications), considered the *Bavli* to be a text shaped by the last editors. A third position, held by David Halivni (2013), highlighted the role of the *stammaim,* writers of the anonymous passages of the *Bavli*. According to him, these rabbis took previous traditions, selected some of them, and rewrote others. This position can be seen as intermediate, because it considers the possible transmission of certain non-re-elaborated fragments, while stressing the influence of the last editors.[12]

So what was Jewish Babylonia like, according to the *Bavli*? First, the text mentions cities and places that allow us to construct a Talmudic geography. The largest Jewish settlements in Mesopotamia were located in the south (Neunser 1965–1970; Gafni 1990). In fact, the most important academies—Nehardea, Mahoza, Sura, and Pumbedita—were in that region. However, Jews also lived in northern cities like Nisibis—before and after the Sassanid conquest—though they were not as numerous as in the south. Another difference between the two regions was the importance of Christianity.[13] In Nisibis, by the fifth century the Christian population outnumbered the Jews. In contrast, Christianity was not demographically significant in the south. Of course, the majority of the population in both regions were neither Christian nor Jewish.

By the time the *Bavli* was edited, rabbis held a hegemonic position in Judaism. Palestinian rabbis, as we have already remarked, gradually imposed their leadership between the second and fourth centuries, but Babylonian rabbis were in a strengthened position. There were non-rabbinical Jews, but in the sixth century most of the Jews had embraced rabbinism. In fact, as Rubenstein (2003, 123–42) points out, the attitude of Babylonian rabbis towards the *am ha'arez* was more violent than that of the Palestinians. Furthermore, Kalmin (2006, 8–9) states that Babylonian rabbis were voluntarily isolated, at least until the fourth century, even inside the Jewish community. In addition, there is a consensus about the influence of rabbis over the entire Jewish population around the sixth century.

The *Bavli* also portrays a good relationship between rabbis and the Sassanid government. Although their relationship with the Parthians was better, the rabbinical movement—beyond certain sporadic and isolated persecutions—maintained cordial relations with the Sassanid court. In fact, the famous dictum "דינא דמלכותא דינא" (the law of the kingdom is the law) was written in the *Bavli* (*b Bava Kamma* 113a, among other places in the *Bavli*).

The Exilarch—a position similar to the Patriarch in the Land of Israel—represented the most direct nexus with the Sassanid government. But the reach of the Exilarch's power is uncertain due to the scarcity of sources. Was the Jewish Babylonian community centralized with the Exilarch at its head? Was he a kind of local governor? Was he similar to the *Catholicos*, the leader of the Christians in Persia? No simple answer can be given (Herman 2012). However, certain facts are unquestionable. The Exilarch was wealthy, he asserted Davidic descendency, and he held certain juridical prerogatives that included the control of prices within the Jewish community. Rabbis—as the *Bavli* reveals—recognized the Exilarch's authority, but also criticized it.

Turning to rabbis, they prioritized the study of and commentary on the Torah. In fact, the emphasis placed on the study of the Torah is greater in the *Bavli* than in the *Yerushalmi*. Rabbis were, of course, the self-proclaimed authorities on analyzing scripture and obtaining laws from it. We are sure that in the Islamic period, the *geonic* academies were at the heart of the rabbinical movement. However, according to the *Talmud*, academies were established earlier. The Sura academy, for example, was founded—in accordance with rabbinical sources—around 225 CE. Nevertheless, as Goodblatt (2006) suggests, the earliest academies—if in fact they existed at that time—were simple organizations, far from the complexity seen in Islamic times. In that sense, during amoraic times, study was centred on masters and their circles of disciples that probably gathered in private houses.

Even though certain scholars have suggested that commerce was the most important rabbinical economic activity, most of the rabbis were involved in agriculture and associated activities. As Gafni (1990, 126–48) stated, even though the *Bavli* contains more text dedicated to commerce than the *Yerushalmi,* this does not mean that rabbis were removed from farming activities. In fact, a serious analysis of the *Bavli* shows that there were many landowners among the rabbis, and others were—directly or indirectly—linked to the agricultural sphere. Of course, there were also artisans and merchants. In that sense the rabbinical movement took part in the same economic activities that the rest of the Jewish and non-Jewish population of the Sassanid Empire did.

It is not easy to reconstruct contacts between rabbis and other religious groups. On the Christian side, as we have seen, there were conflicts with Jews. However, Babylonian rabbinic literature left few traces of that controversy. Jesus, Christians, and Christianity were given no more than twelve direct mentions in the whole *Bavli.* It is true that references to Jesus or the even more ascetic "goyim" were censored in the late Middle Ages and in early modernity. Nevertheless, even manuscripts prior to the Christian censorship (and Jewish self-censorship) show that Christianity was not a central concern for Babylonian rabbis.[14] This is coherent with the context we have described: a limited Christian community in Babylonia and a self-confident rabbinical movement in the region.

When the Parthian dynasty was replaced by the Sassanid, Zoroastrianism acquired a major position in the new empire. Indeed, *magi* affected some parts of Jewish life. Disruptions were centred on ritual issues related to Zoroastrian religiosity.[15] For example, in Zoroastrianism bodies cannot be buried due to the purity of the soil (examples in *b Bava Bathra* 58a, and *b Yevamoth* 63b), and ritual immersion in *mikvaot* was also prohibited (for example, *b Yevamot* 63b). In addition, fire was sacred for Zoroastrianism and the *Bavli* describes tensions around this too (see *b Gittin* 16b–17a). However, it is important to highlight that attempts to convert Jews to Zoroastrianism are not detected in the rabbinic literature.

Furthermore, beyond those disruptions it is possible to detect a positive attitude, not only toward the government but also toward Persians and Zoroastrianism. For example, the *Bavli* stated that weapons could not be sold to any non-Jews, except Persians (*b Avoda Zara* 16a). In addition, Jews and Persians exchanged gifts according to *b Arakhin* 6b, and the situation of a Jew and a Zoroastrian sharing the same house is described—or imagined—in *b Avoda Zara* 70a (Gafni 2002). There was also an implicit admiration of Persian purity norms. According to Yaacov Elman (2007a and 2007b), certain regulations in the *Bavli* regarding menstruation were heavily influenced by Zoroastrian norms. In fact, the *Bavli* should be understood in its Iranian context, because not only purity norms but also other cultural aspects were adopted from the Persians.[16] It is important to keep in mind that there were also western influences on the text—mainly from Palestine—through the *Yerushalmi* but also as a result of frequent trips between both regions.

As we have seen, being a non-rabbinical Jew in Babylonia was more difficult than in Palestine. The rabbinical approach towards *am ha'aretz* is, in fact, worse in the *Bavli* than in the *Yerushalmi*. Certainly, *am ha'aretz* as a concept does not necessarily imply non-rabbinical or opposition to rabbis. However, people not involved in rabbinical discussions and resolutions were regarded by the rabbis as uneducated. Indeed, sometimes the voices of the common people can be heard in the *Bavli*.[17] Non-rabbis are, however, absent from our history. Even though we could imagine them using magic bowls or going to synagogues, no literature depicts them beyond a caricature.

Notes

[1] On the *Bavli*, see Neusner 1987, Kalmin 1994, and Halivni 2013, among others.

[2] On archaeology in Jewish Babylonia, see Geller 2015.

[3] Jewish seals were compiled by Friedenberg 2009.

[4] It is interesting that the *Bavli* does mention the *menorah* on different occasions. Interestingly, there is a Babylonian prohibition—not found in *Yerushalmi*—against reproducing the *menorah* (for example, *b Avoda Zara* 43a), but it can be understood as a ban on making a reproduction and not a depiction. On debates around this prohibition, see Hachlili 2001, 200–31. Obviously, more archaeological evidence is needed.

[5] Compilation and commentaries of Jewish incantation bowls, in Naveh and Shaked 1993, Levene 2003, and Shaked et al. 2013. For an interesting approach to Sassanian incantation bowls, see Morony 2007.

[6] As we stated previously, a name does not always indicate religion. Notwithstanding, it is an important identity marker.

[7] However, as Juusola (1999) asserted, language and religion do not always match. Thus, certain incantation bowls written in Syriac—a dialect most commonly used by Christians—contained Jewish texts and were apparently used by Jews.

[8] *Hekhalot* literature are late ancient and early medieval Jewish texts related to mysticism. See Schäfer 2010.

[9] According to a recent article written by Shaked (2015), "rabbis" in magic bowls were effectively Talmudic rabbis. He analyzes an incantation bowl, where Rav Ashi is mentioned as the owner, concluding that "The bowl made for Rav Ashi son of Maḥlafta, may have been made for this person" (103).

[10] There are certain references attacking the Jews in the Skand-Gumanik Vicar, a text written in the ninth century, which probably collected earlier written traditions. See Neusner 1986, 175–95.

[11] On Aphrahat and the Jews, see Koltun-Fromm 2012, and Lizorkin-Eyzenberg 2012.

[12] Nevertheless, it is important to highlight that there is no consensus around the role—and even the existence—of the *stammaim*.

[13] Nestorian Christianity was very important in the area after the fifth century.

[14] On Jesus and Christianity in the *Bavli*, see Schäfer 2007, Murcia 2014. See also Laham Cohen 2016 and 2017.

[15] On Jews and Zoroastrianism, see Neusner 1986, Gafni 2002, and Elman 2007a and 2007b.

[16] For example, according to Elman (2007b, 181), Huna bar Nathan used the Zoroastrian belt, the *Kustig*. For the *Bavli* and the Iranian context, see Bakhos and Shayegan 2010.

[17] In *b Sanhedrin* 99a an *epikoros*—a term that can be translated as "Epicurean," although that is not the exact meaning—challenged the role of the rabbis. He stated that they read and studied the Torah only for their own benefit.

Afterword

Over the course of these pages we have tried to elaborate on a snapshot of Jewish communities in late antiquity. Due to space concerns, we have not been able to analyze significant Jewish settlements in Syria, Asia Minor, and the Balkans. However, the scope of the regions studied have given a broad view of Judaism in the period.

We have showed the importance of all types of sources when reconstructing Jewish life, namely buildings, artifacts, inscriptions, and Jewish and non-Jewish texts. As we are dealing with groups that left scant traces, it is important to employ all the available evidence.

Is it possible to summarize the history of the Jews in late antiquity? As we have seen, our knowledge is imperfect because of the insufficiency of sources. In Italy, we depend heavily on Christian sources, although there are two uncovered ancient synagogues, while in Babylonia there are many Jewish texts, but no significant archaeological remains. In Gaul, only a few inscriptions are available and, again, Christian texts, while in Spain (Christian) legal codes are almost the only avenue available to us in order to find out about the Jews. This disparity of sources makes it difficult to compare distinct regions. As no Jewish texts survived in Western Europe, uncovering the scope of the rabbinization process in the region is a difficult task.

The absence of archaeological remains—apart from seals and magic bowls—in Babylonia, makes it hard to contrast the imagined rabbinical society with material sources. Only in the Land of Israel are there a variety of sources that provide a relatively complete view. Nevertheless, even in Palestine, scholars continue to engage in fierce debates around certain issues, such as the strength of the Patriarch or the involvement of the rabbinical movement in the synagogues, among other aspects.

No less important, we know more about the elites than we do about the common people. As is often the case in ancient and medieval times, constructing history from below is not always possible: poor people in antiquity did not have seals, did not always make tombstones for their deaths, and generally did not write (or their texts were not preserved).

Was there a common Judaism in late antiquity? The answer is not straightforward. There are certain patterns that could be compared. For example, artistic motifs such as *menorah*, *lulav*, or *etrog* are found in the archaeological remains of Italy, Gaul, North Africa, and Palestine. The improvement of the space for the Torah can be seen in several regions. There is also evidence of rabbinical influence in southern Italy from the sixth century onward and even earlier in North Africa. We also know the final result: the almost complete rabbinization of the Diaspora by the ninth century. Furthermore, Palestinian Judaism was re-rabbinized by Babylonian Judaism in the early Middle Ages.

On the other hand, there were also differences between the regions. The iconography of synagogues and cemeteries, beyond the specific Jewish repertoire, featured art shared with other religious groups of every region. Even architectural features were influenced by the designs specific to each location. Although Jewish culture in Europe—due to the absence of Jewish texts—is difficult to analyze, both *Talmudim* show Roman, Christian, and Persian influences.

No less important, political and religious concerns also impacted the development of Jewish communities: the empowerment of Christianity in the Roman Empire was critical for Jewish settlements inside it. In contrast, Zoroastrians overall were more moderate than Christians. However, Christianity was not uniform and that reality also affected the Jews. Thus, Jews living in Gaul were in a better position than Jews under the Visigoths. Moreover, even within a single region, the position of the religious elite influenced the policy toward Jews. As we saw in Italy, Jews living in Terracina were expelled twice from their synagogue whilst only one hundred kilometres north, in Rome, Jews were protected by the Pope.

Further Reading

The following (brief) annotated list presents titles already mentioned and/or cited in the book. The list is not meant to be comprehensive, but we have selected these titles because they are central to understanding key features of the Jewish history in late antiquity.

General

Dohrmann, Natalie, and Annette Yoshiko Reed, eds. *Jews, Christians, and the Roman Empire: The Poetics of Power in Late Antiquity*. Philadelphia: University of Pennsylvania Press, 2013.

> A fundamental compilation of chapters regarding different aspects of Jewish history in late antiquity.

Fine, Steven. *Art & Judaism in the Greco-Roman World: Toward a New Jewish Archaeology*. Cambridge: Cambridge University Press, 2005.

> Clever, far-reaching, and in some ways polemical, this book studies not only late ancient Jewish art and architecture but also contemporary visions on those topics.

Hachlili, Rachel. *Ancient Synagogues. Archaeology and Art: New Discoveries and Current Research*. Leiden: Brill, 2013.

> An excellent, comprehensive, and actualized survey of the ancient synagogues in Israel and the Diaspora.

Katz, Steven, ed. *The Cambridge History of Judaism*. Vol. 4: The Late Roman-Rabbinic Period. Cambridge: Cambridge University Press, 2006.

> An essential collection of chapters related to Judaism between the first century and seventh century CE.

Levine, Lee. *The Ancient Synagogue: The First Thousand Years*. New Haven: Yale University Press, 2005.

> A clear and ample book in which the origin and development of the synagogue is studied.

Van der Horst, Pieter. *Saxa Judaica Loquuntur: Lessons from Early Jewish Inscriptions*. Leiden: Brill, 2014.

> Van der Horst shows all the possibilities that ancient Jewish epigraphy offers to improve our knowledge about the period.

Italy

Cappelletti, Silvia. *The Jewish Community of Rome: From the Second Century BC to the Third Century CE*. Leiden: Brill, 2006.

> Investigates textual, epigraphic, and archaeological sources in order to reconstruct the Jewish life in Rome in antiquity.

Rutgers, Leonard. *The Jews in Late Ancient Rome: Evidence of Cultural Interaction in the Roman Diaspora*. Leiden: Brill, 1995.

> Rutgers's view emphasizes the interaction between Jews, Christians, and pagans in late antiquity thanks to a comprehensive study of textual, epigraphic, and archaeological sources.

Simonsohn, Shlomo. *The Jews of Italy: Antiquity*. Leiden: Brill, 2014.

> A long-range analysis of the Jewish settlement in Rome between the Republic and Gregory the Great.

North Africa

Binder, Stephanie. *Tertullian, On Idolatry, and Mishnah Avodah Zarah: Questioning the Parting of the Ways between Christians and Jews*. Leiden: Brill, 2012.

> A very interesting work that attempts to understand the relationship between Jews and Christians in North Africa, comparing Tertullian's *On Idolatry* and *m Avoda Zara*.

Fredriksen, Paula. *Augustine and the Jews: A Christian Defense of Jews and Judaism*. New York: Doubleday, 2008.

> A deep analysis on Augustine's texts allows Fredriksen to reconstruct and rethink Anti-Judaism and Augustinian positions on Jews.

Stern, Karen. *Inscribing Devotion and Death: Archaeological Evidence for Jewish Populations of North Africa*. Leiden: Brill, 2008.

> An excellent investigation of archaeological and epigraphic Jewish evidence in North Africa.

Gaul

Boddens Hosang, Elizabeth. *Establishing Boundaries Christian-Jewish Relations in Early Council Texts and the Writings of Church Fathers*. Leiden: Brill, 2010.

> Boddens Hosang examines the way in which early councils tried to shape Christian and Jewish identities. She also shows how councils help to understand the relationship between Jews and Christians in late antiquity, mainly in Gaul.

Wood, Ian, and Kathleen Mitchell, eds. *The World of Gregory of Tours*. Leiden: Brill, 2002.

> Although we only cited the excellent work of Emily Rose on the conversion of the Jews of Clermont, the entire book offers hints to understand the Merovingian world.

Spain

Drews, Wolfram. *The Unknown Neighbour: The Jew in the Thought of Isidore of Seville*. Leiden: Brill, 2006.

> An excellent analysis of the role of the Jew in the discourse of Isidore of Seville and its implications.

González Salinero, Raúl. *Las conversiones forzosas de los judíos en el reino visigodo*. Roma: Escuela Española de Roma, 2000b.

> Probably the best work on the situation of the Jews in late ancient Spain.

Egypt

Gruen, Erich. *Diaspora: Jews amidst Greeks and Romans*. Cambridge: Harvard University Press, 2002.

> Although Gruen's book explores the Jewish communities of Rome, Alexandria, and the Roman province of Asia, we specially recommend the chapter on the Jews of Alexandria.

Haas, Christopher. *Alexandria in Late Antiquity: Topography and Social Conflict*. Baltimore: Johns Hopkins University Press, 1997.

Haas investigates the situation in Alexandria in late antiquity, remarking on the interaction between religious communities. An entire chapter examines the condition of the Jews in the city.

The Land of Israel

Hezser, Catherine, ed. *The Oxford Handbook of Jewish Daily Life in Roman Palestine*. Oxford: Oxford University Press, 2010.

A fundamental compilation of chapters on different aspects of Jewish daily life in late ancient Palestine. Hezser's methodological chapter is essential.

Schwartz, Seth. *Imperialism and Jewish Society: 200 B.C.E. to 640 C.E.* Princeton: Princeton University Press, 2001.

Schwartz's book gives a new outlook on late ancient Jewish history of the Land of Israel. Even though his conclusions are polemical, reading the book remains crucial.

Sivan, Hagith, *Palestine in Late Antiquity*. Oxford: Oxford University Press, 2008.

A comprehensive and enjoyable book on Jewish and non-Jewish history of Palestine in late antiquity

Babylonia

Gafni, Isaiah. *The Jews of Babylonia in the Talmudic Era: A Social and Cultural History*. Jerusalem: Zalman Shazar Center for Jewish History, 1990 (Hebrew).

A fundamental book on the history of the Jews in Mesopotamia during late antiquity.

Halivni, David. *The Formation of the Babylonian Talmud*. New York: Oxford University Press, 2013.

An actualized (and polemical) book concerning the edition (who? when? how?) of the Babylonian Talmud.

Kalmin, Richard. *Jewish Babylonia between Persia and Roman Palestine: Decoding the Literary Record*. New York: Oxford University Press, 2006.

Examines the history of the Jews of Babylonia, analyzing rabbinic literature and trying to understand the relationship with Christian and Persian cultures.

Bibliography

The aim of this book was to concisely present facts and debates around Jews in late antiquity. If the reader feels they need more material, we have accomplished our task. This book is just the first step.

Albert, Bat-Sheva. "Isidore of Seville: His Attitude Towards Judaism and His Impact on Early Medieval Canon Law." *The Jewish Quarterly Review* 80 (1990): 207–20.

Alexander, Philip. "Using Rabbinic Literature as a Source for the History of Late Roman Palestine: Problems and Issues." In *Rabbinic Texts and the History of Late Roman Palestine*, edited by Martin Goodman and Philip Alexander, 7–24. Oxford: Oxford University Press, 2010.

Ameling, Walter et al. *Corpus Inscriptionum Iudaeae Palaestinae. A Multi-lingual Corpus of the Inscriptions from Alexander to Muhammad.* Vols. 2–3: *Caesarea and the Middle Coast; South Coast.* Berlin: De Gruyter, 2012–2014.

Avi-Yonah, Michael. *The Jews of Palestine: A Political History from the Bar Kokhba War to the Arab Conquest.* Oxford: Blackwell, 1976.

Bakhos, Carol, and Rahim Shayean. *The Talmud in its Iranian Context.* Tübingen: Mohr Siebeck, 2010.

Baron, Salo. "Ghetto and Emancipation: Shall We Revise the Traditional View?" *Menorah* 14 (1928): 515–26.

Benveniste, Henriette. "On the Language of Conversion: Visigothic Spain Revisited." *Historein* 6 (2006): 72–87.

Bleiberg, Edward. "Art and Assimilation: The Floor Mosaics from the Synagogue at Hammam Lif." In *Age of Transition: Byzantine Culture in the Islamic World*, edited by Helen Evans, 30–37. New Heaven: Yale University Press, 2015.

Blumenkranz, Bernhard. *Les auteurs chrétiens du Moyen Age sur les juifs et le judaïsme.* Paris: Mouton, 1963.

Bohak, Gideon. *Ancient Jewish Magic. A History.* Cambridge: Cambridge University Press, 2008.

Boustan, Ra'anan, and Joseph Sanzo. "Christian Magicians, Jewish Magical Idioms, and the Shared Magical Culture of Late Antiquity." *Harvard Theological Review* 110 (2017): 217–40.

Boyarin, Daniel. "The Christian Invention of Judaism: The Theodosian Empire and the Rabbinic Refusal of Religion." *Representations* 85 (2004): 21–57.

———. *Dying for God: Martyrdom and the Making of Christianity and Judaism.* Stanford: Stanford University Press, 1999.

Brown, Peter. *The World of Late Antiquity: From Marcus Aurelius to Muhammad.* London: Thames and Hudson, 1971.

Carleton Paget, James. "Clement of Alexandria and the Jews." *Scottish Journal of Theology* 51 (1998): 86–97.

Cohen, Jeremy. *Living Letters of the Law: Ideas of the Jew in Medieval Christianity.* Berkeley: University of California Press, 1999.

Cohen, Shaye. "Epigraphical Rabbis." *The Jewish Quarterly Review* 72 (1981): 1–17.

Colafemmina, Cesare. "Hebrew Inscriptions of the Early Medieval Period in Southern Italy." In *The Jews of Italy: Memory and Identity*, edited by Bernard Cooperman and Barbara Garvin, 65–81. Potomac: University Press of Maryland, 2000.

Colorni, Vittore. *L'uso del greco nella liturgia del giudaismo elenistico e la Novella 146 di Giustiniano.* Milan: Giuffre, 1964.

Costamagna, Liliana. "La sinagoga di Bova Marina." In *I beni culturali ebraici in Italia: situazione attuale, problemi, prospettive e progetti per il futuro*, edited by Mauro Perani, 93–118. Ravenna: Longo Angelo, 2003.

Cotton, Hannah. "Change and Continuity in Late Legal Papyri from Palaestina Tertia. *Nomos Hellênikos* and *Ethos Rômaikon*." In *Jews, Christians, and the Roman Empire: The Poetics of Power in Late Antiquity*, edited by Natalie Dohrmann and Annette Yoshiko Reed, 209–21. Philadelphia: University of Pennsylvania Press, 2013.

Cotton, Hannah et al. *Corpus Inscriptionum Iudaeae/Palaestinae: A Multi-lingual Corpus of the Inscriptions from Alexander to Muhammad.* Vol. 1: *Jerusalem.* Berlin: De Gruyter, 2010.

Dagron, Gilbert, and Vincent Déroche. *Juifs et chrétiens en Orient byzantin.* Paris: Association des amis du Centre d'histoire et civilisation de Byzance, 2010.

Dauphin, Claudine. *La Palestine byzantine: peuplement et populations.* Oxford: Archaeopress, 1998.

De Bonfils, Giovanni. *Gli schiavi dagli ebrei nella legislazione del IV secolo: storia di un divieto.* Bari: Cacucci, 1992.

De Lange, Nicholas. *Origen and the Jews: Studies in Jewish Christian Relations in Third-Century Palestine.* Cambridge: Cambridge University Press, 1978.

Del Valle Rodríguez, Carlos. "San Julián de Toledo." In *La controversia judeocristiana en España (desde los orígenes hasta el siglo XIII): Homenaje a Domingo Muñoz León,* edited by Carlos Del Valle Rodríguez, 115–18. Madrid: CSIC, 1998.

Dönitz, Saskia. "Historiography among Byzantine Jews—the Case of Sefer Yosippon." In *Jews in Byzantium: Dialectics of Minority and Majority Cultures,* edited by Robert Bonfil et al., 953–70. Leiden: Brill, 2012.

Drake, Susanna. *Slandering the Jew: Sexuality and Difference in Early Christian Texts.* Philadelphia: University of Pennsylvania Press, 2013.

Dunn, Geoffrey. *Tertullian's Adversus Iudaeos: A Rethorical Analysis.* Washington: Catholic University of America Press, 2008.

Efroymson, David. "The Patristic Connection." In *Antisemitism and the Foundations of Christianity,* edited by Alan Davies, 98–117. New York: Paulist, 1979.

———. "Two Augustines?" *Expositions* 3 (2009): 209–14.

Elman, Yaakov. " 'He in his Cloak and She in her Cloak': Conflicting Images of Sexuality in Sasanian Mesopotamia." In *Discussing Cultural Influences: Text, Context, and Non-Text in Rabbinic Judaism,* edited by Rivka Ulmer, 129–63. Maryland: University Press of America, 2007b.

———. "Middle Persian Culture and Babylonian Sages: Accommodation and Resistance in the Shaping of Rabbinic Legal Tradition." In *The Cambridge Companion to the Talmud and Rabbinic Literature,* edited by Charlotte Fonrobert and Martin Jaffee, 165–97. Cambridge: Cambridge University Press, 2007a.

Elsner, Jas. "Archaeologies and Agendas: Reflections on Late Ancient Jewish Art and Early Christian Art." *Journal of Roman Studies* 93 (2003): 115–28.

Fine, Steven. *Art, History and the Historiography of Judaism in Roman Antiquity.* Leiden: Brill, 2014.

———. *Art and Judaism in the Greco-Roman World: Toward a New Jewish Archaeology.* Cambridge: Cambridge University Press, 2005.

———. "Death, Burial, and Afterlife." In *The Oxford Handbook of Jewish Daily Life in Roman Palestine*, edited by Catherine Hezser, 440–64. Oxford: Oxford University Press, 2010.

Frakes, Robert. *Compiling* the Collatio Legum Mosaicarum et Romanarum *in Late Antiquity.* Oxford: Oxford University Press, 2011.

Fredriksen, Paula. "Roman Christianity and the Post-Roman West: The Social Correlates of the *Contra Iudaeos* Tradition." In *Jews, Christians, and the Roman Empire: The Poetics of Power in Late Antiquity*, edited by Natalie Dohrmann and Annette Yoshiko Reed, 249–66. Philadelphia: University of Pennsylvania Press, 2013.

Fredriksen, Paula, and Oded Irshai. "Christian Anti-Judaism: Polemics and Policies." In *The Cambridge History of* Judaism, edited by Steven Katz, vol. 4, 977–1034. Cambridge: Cambridge University Press, 2006.

Frey, Jean-Baptiste. *Corpus Inscriptionum Judaicarum*. Vol. 2. Vatican City: Pontificio Istituto di Archeologia Cristiana (= CIJ), 1952.

Friedenberg, Daniel. *Sasanian Jewry and its Culture: A Lexicon of Jewish and Related Seals.* Urbana: University of Illinois Press, 2009.

Friedheim, Emmanuel. *Rabbinisme et paganisme en Palestine romaine: Étude historique des* Realia *talmudiques* (Ier-IVème siècles). Leiden: Brill, 2006.

Gafni, Isaiah. "Babylonian Rabbinic Culture." In *Culture of the Jews: A New History*, edited by David Biale, 225–65. New York: Schocken Books, 2002.

Geisel, Christof. *Die Juden im Frankenreich: Von den Merowingern bis zum Tode Ludwigs des Frommen.* Frankfurt: Peter Lang, 1998.

Geller, Markham. *The Archaeology and Material Culture of the Babylonian Talmud.* Leiden: Brill, 2015.

Goffart, Walter. "The Conversions of Avitus of Clermont and Similar Passages in Gregory of Tours." In *Rome's Fall and After*, 293–317. London: Hambledon Press, 1989.

González Salinero, Raúl. *El antijudaísmo cristiano occidental (siglos IV y V)*. Madrid: Trotta, 2000a.

———. "Los judíos en el reino visigodo de época arriana: consideraciones sobre un largo debate." In *Judaísmo hispano: Estudios en memoria de José Luis Lacave Riaño*, edited by Elena Romero, 399–408. Madrid: CSIC, 2002.

———. "Preaching and Jews in Late Antiquity and Visigothic Iberia." In *The Jewish-Christian Encounter in Medieval Preaching*, edited by Jonathan Adams and Jussi Hanska, 23–58. New York: Routledge, 2015.

Goodblatt, David. "The History of the Babylonian Academies." In *The Cambridge History of Judaism, vol.* 4, edited by Steven Katz, 821–39. Cambridge: Cambridge University Press, 2006.

Hachlili, Rachel. *Ancient Jewish Art and Archaeology in the Diaspora*. Leiden: Brill, 1998.

———. *The Menorah, the Ancient Seven-Armed Candelabrum: Origin, Form and Significance*. Leiden: Brill, 2001.

Hadas-Lebel, Mireille. *Philo of Alexandria: A Thinker in the Jewish Diaspora*. Leiden: Brill, 2012.

Handley, Mark. " 'This stone shall be a witness' (Joshua 24.27): Jews, Christians and Inscriptions in Early Medieval Gaul." In *Christian-Jewish Relations through the Centuries,* edited by Stanley Porter and Brook Pearson, 239–54. Sheffield: Sheffield Academic Press, 2000.

Harviainen, Tapani. "An Aramaic Incantation Bowl from Borsippa: Another Specimen of Eastern Aramaic 'Koiné'." *Studia Orientalia* 51 (1981): 3–29.

Heil, Johannes. "Agobard, Amolo, das Kirchengut und die Juden von Lyon." *Forschungen zur westeuropäischen Geschichte* 25 (1998): 39–76.

———. "Die Konstruktion der Hispanisch-Jüdischen Geschichte der ersten Jahrhunderte: ein Versuch." *Temas Medievales* 25 (2017): 39–61.

Herman, Geoffrey. *A Prince without a Kingdom: The Exilarch in the Sasanian Era*. Tübingen: Mohr Siebeck, 2012.

Hezser, Catherine. "Correlating Literary, Epigraphic, and Archaeological Sources." In *The Oxford Handbook of Jewish Daily Life in Roman Palestine*, edited by Catherine Hezser, 9–27. Oxford: Oxford University Press, 2010.

———. "The (In)Significance of Jerusalem in the Talmud Yerushalmi.' In *The Talmud Yerushalmi and Graeco Roman Culture*, edited by Catherine Hezser and Peter Schäfer, vol. 3, 11–49. Tübingen: Mohr Siebeck, 2000.

———. *The Social Structure of the Rabbinic Movement in Roman Palestine*. Tübingen: Mohr Siebeck, 1997.

Horbury, William. "Tertullian on the Jews in the Light of *De Spectaculis* XXX, 5–6." In *Jews and Christians: In Contact and Controversy*, edited by William Horbury, 176–79. Edinburgh: T&T Clark, 1998.

Horbury, William, and David Noy. *Jewish Inscriptions of Graeco-Roman Egypt*. Cambridge: Cambridge University Press, 1993 (= JIGRE).

Ilan, Tal. "The Jewish Community in Egypt before and After 117 CE in Light of Old and New Papyri." In *Jewish and Christian Communal Identities in the Roman World*, edited by Yair Furstenberg, 201–24. Leiden: Brill, 2016.

———. *Lexicon of Jewish Names in Late Antiquity, p. III: The Western Diaspora 330 BCE—650 CE*. Tübingen: Mohr Siebeck, 2008.

Irshai, Oded. "Christian Historiographer's Reflection on Jewish Christian Violence in Fifth-Century Alexandria." In *Jews, Christians, and the Roman Empire: The Poetics of Power in Late Antiquity*, edited by Natalie Dohrmann and Annette Yoshiko Reed, 137–53. Philadelphia: University of Pennsylvania Press, 2013.

Juusola, Hannu. "Who Wrote the Syriac Incantation Bowls?" *Studia Orientalia* 85 (1999): 75–92.

Kalmin, Richard. *Sages, Stories, Authors, and Editors in Rabbinic Babylonia*. Atlanta: Scholars Press, 1994.

Keely, Avril. "Arians and Jews in the Histories of Gregory of Tours." *Journal of Medieval History* 23 (1997): 103–15.

Kerkeslager, Allen. "The Jews in Egypt and Cyrenaica 66–c. 235 CE." In *The Cambridge History of Judaism*, edited by Steven Katz, vol. 4, 53–68. Cambridge: Cambridge University Press, 2006.

Koltun-Fromm, Naomi. *Jewish-Christian Conversation in Fourth-Century Persian Mesopotamia: A Reconstructed Conversation*. Piscataway: Gorgias Press, 2012.

Kraemer, David. *The Meanings of Death in Rabbinic Judaism*. New York: Routledge, 2001.

Laham Cohen, Rodrigo. "La confusión como estrategia retórica. María y Jesús en *b Shabbat* 104b y *b Sanedrín* 67a." *Antiquité Tardive* 24 (2016): 285–303.

——. "Entre la represión y la tolerancia. El derrotero de los judíos en tiempos de Gregorio Magno e Isidoro de Sevilla." *Trabajos y Comunicaciones* 36 (2010): 13–35.

——. *Judíos hermenéuticos y judíos históricos en tiempos de Gregorio Magno*. Buenos Aires: Universidad de Buenos Aires, 2013a (PhD thesis).

——. "Los judíos en el *Registrum epistularum* de Gregorio Magno y la epigrafía judía de los siglos VI y VII." *Henoch* 35 (2013b): 214–46.

——. "La mirada atrevida: Jesús en b Sanedrín 107b y la tópica *Adversus Iudaeos*." *Annali di Storia dell'Esegesi* 34 (2017): 577–602.

——. "Theological Anti-Judaism in Gregory the Great." *Sefarad* 75 (2015a): 225–52.

——. "*Vas uacuum et signatum*: La imagen del judío en los *Dialogi* y el problema de la autoría gregoriana." *Revue des Études Juives* 174 (2015b): 295–324.

Laham Cohen, Rodrigo, and Carolina Pecznik. "*Iudaei et Iudaei baptizati* en la ley de los visigodos." *Anuario de la Escuela de Historia* 28 (2016): 141–69.

Langenwalter, Anna. *Agobard of Lyon: An Exploration of Carolingian Jewish-Christian Relations*. Toronto: University of Toronto, 2010 (PhD thesis).

Lapin, Hayim. "Epigraphical Rabbis: A Reconsideration." *Jewish Quarterly Review* 101 (2011): 311–46.

——. *Rabbis as Romans: The Rabbinic Movement in Palestine, 100–400 CE*. Oxford: Oxford University Press, 2012.

Le Bohec, Yann. "Inscriptions juives et judaïsantes de l'Afrique romaine." *Antiquités Africaines* 17 (1981a): 165–207.

——. "Juifs et judaïsantes dans l'Afrique: Remarques onomastiques." *Antiquités Africaines* 17 (1981b): 209–29.

Levene, Dan. *A Corpus of Magic Bowls: Incantation Texts in Jewish Aramaic*. London: Kegan Paul, 2003.

Levine, Lee. *The Galilee in Late Antiquity.* New York: Jewish Theological Seminary of America, 1992.

Linder, Amnon. *The Jews in the Legal Sources of the Early Middle Ages.* Detroit: Wayne State University Press, 1997.

———. *The Jews in Roman Imperial Legislation.* Detroit: Wayne State University Press, 1987.

Lizorkin-Eyzenberg, Eliyahu. *Aphrahat's Demonstrations: A Conversation with the Jews of Mesopotamia.* Leuven: Peeters, 2012.

Lund, John. "A Synagogue at Carthage? Menorah-lamps from the Danish Excavations." *Journal of Roman Archaeology* 8 (1995): 245–62.

Mancuso, Piergabriele. *Shabbatai Donnolo's Sefer Hakhmoni.* Leiden: Brill, 2010.

Markus, Robert. *Gregory the Great and his World.* Cambridge: Cambridge University Press, 1997.

Martin, Celine, and Capucine Nemo-Pekelman. "Les Juifs et la cité: Pour une clarification du statut personnel des juifs de l'Antiquité Tardive à la fin du Royaume de Tolède (IVe-VIIe siècles)." *Antiquité Tardive* 16 (2008): 1–24.

Martínez Díez, Gustavo, and Félix Rodríguez. *La colección canónica hispana.* Vol. 5. Madrid: CSIC, 1992.

Massie, Alban. *Peuple prophétique et nation témoin: Le peuple juif dans le* Contra Faustum manichaeum *de saint Augustin.* Paris: Institut d'Études Augustiniennes, 2011.

Meerson, Michael, and Peter Schäfer. *Toledot Yeshu: The Life Story of Jesus.* Tübingen: Mohr Siebeck, 2014.

Meyers, Eric. "The Use of Archaeology in Understanding Rabbinic Materials: An Archaeological Perspective." In *Talmuda de-Eretz Israel: Archaeology and the Rabbis in Late Antique Palestine,* edited by Steven Fine and Aaron Koller, 303–19. Berlin: De Gruyter, 2014.

Milson, David. *Art and Architecture of the Synagogue in Late Antique Palestine: In the Shadow of the Church.* Boston: Brill, 2007.

Morony, Michael. "Religion and the Aramaic Incantation Bowls." *Religion Compass* 1 (2007): 414–29.

Murcia, Thierry. *Jésus dans le Talmud et la littérature rabbinique ancienne.* Turnhout: Brepols, 2014.

Murphy, Frederick. *Pseudo-Philo: Rewriting the Bible.* Oxford: Oxford University Press, 1993.

Nauroy, Gérard. "Ambrose et la question juive à Milan à la fin du IVe siècle: Une nouvelle lecture de l'*Epistula* 74 (=40) à Théodose." In *Les chrétiens face à leurs adversaires dans l'Occident latin au IVe siècle*, edited by Jean-Michel Poinsotte, 37–59. Rouen: Publications de l'Université de Rouen, 2001.

Naveh, Joseph, and Shaul Shaked. *Magic Spells and Formulae: Aramaic Incantations of Late Antiquity.* Jerusalem: Magnes Press, 1993.

Nemo-Pekelman, Capuciñe. *Rome et ses citoyens juifs (IVe-Ve siècles).* Paris: Honoré Champion, 2010.

Neusner, Jacob. *The Bavli and its Sources: The Question of Tradition in the Case of Tractate Sukkah.* Atlanta: Scholars Press, 1987.

———. *A History of the Jews of Babylonia.* Leiden: Brill, 1965–1970.

———. *Judaism, Christianity and Zoroastrianism in Talmudic Babylonia.* Lanham: University Press of America, 1986.

Nickelsburg, George. *Jewish Literature between the Bible and the Mishnah.* Minneapolis: Fortress Press, 2005.

Niehoff, Maren. "A Jewish Critique of Christianity from Second-Century Alexandria: Revisiting the Jew Mentioned in *Contra Celsum*." *Journal of Early Christian Studies* 21 (2013): 151–75.

Noy, David, *Jewish Inscriptions of Western Europe.* Vol. 1: *Italy (excluding the city of Rome), Spain and Gaul.* Cambridge: Cambridge University Press, 1993 (= 1 JIWE).

———. *Jewish Inscriptions of Western Europe.* Vol. 2: *Rome.* Cambridge: Cambridge University Press, 1995 (= 2 JIWE).

Olsson, Birger. *The Synagogue of Ancient Ostia and the Jews of Rome. Interdisciplinary Studies.* Stockholm: Paul Åströms, 2001.

Pakter, William. *Medieval Canon Law and the Jews.* Ebelsbach: Rolf Gremer, 1988.

Poveda Navarro, Antonio. "El edificio de culto de "La Ancudia" de Elche: ¿sinagoga o basílica? Un siglo de debates." In *¿Una Sefarad inventada? Los problemas de interpretación de los restos materiales de los judíos en España*, edited by Javier Castaño, 161–79. Córdoba: El Almendro, 2014.

Rabello, Alfredo. *Giustiniano, ebrei e samaritani alla luce delle fonti storico-letterarie, ecclesiastiche e giuridiche.* Milán: Giuffrè, 1988.

———. "Justinian and the Revision of Jewish Legal Status." In *The Cambridge History of Judaism,* edited by Steven Katz, vol. 4, 1073–77. Cambridge: Cambridge University Press, 2006.

Rajak, Tessa. *Translation and Survival: The Greek Bible of the Ancient Jewish Diaspora.* Oxford: Oxford University Press, 2009.

Ramelli, Ilaria. "L'Epistola Anne ad Senecam de superbia et idolis: Documento pseudo-epigrafico probabilmente cristiano." *Augustinianum* 44 (2004): 25–50.

Ribak, Eliya. *Religious Communities in Byzantine Palestine: The Relationship between Judaism, Christianity and Islam, AD 400–700.* Oxford: Archaeopress, 2007.

Rodgers, Zuleika. *Making History: Josephus and Historical Method.* Leiden: Brill, 2007.

Rose, Emily. "Gregory of Tours and the Conversion of the Jews of Clermont." In *The World of Gregory of Tours,* edited by Ian Wood and Kathleen Mitchell, 307–20. Leiden: Brill, 2002.

Rosenberg, Stephen. "The Jewish Temple at Elephantine." *Near Eastern Archaeology* 67 (2004): 4–13.

Rosenblum, Jordan. *Food and Identity in Early Rabbinic Judaism.* Cambridge: Cambridge University Press, 2010.

Rouche, Michel. "Les baptêmes forcés de juifs en Gaule Mérovingienne et dans l'Empire Romain d'Orient." In *Le choc des cultures: Romanité, germanité, chrétienté durant le Haut Moyen Âge,* edited by Jean Heuclin, 223–42. Villeneuve d'Ascq: Presses Universitaires Du Septentrion, 2003.

Rubenstein, Geoffrey. *The Culture of the Babylonian Talmud.* Baltimore: Johns Hopkins University Press, 2003.

Ruether, Rosemary. *Faith and Fratricide: The Theological Roots of Anti-Semitism.* New York: Seabury Press, 1974.

Rutgers, Leonard. "Justinian's Novella 146 between Jews and Christian." In *Making Myths: Jews in Early Christian Identity Formation,* edited by Leonard Rutgers, 49–77. Leuven: Peeters, 2009.

Safrai, Zeev. "The Communal Functions of the Synagogue in the Land of Israel in the Rabbinic Period." In *Ancient Synagogues: Historical*

Analysis and Archaeological Discovery, edited by Dan Urman and Paul Flesher, 181–204. Leiden: Brill, 1995.

Schäfer, Peter. "Hekhalot Literature and the Origins of Jewish Mysticism." In *Rabbinic Texts and the History of Late Roman Palestine,* edited by Martin Goodman and Philip Alexander, 265–80. Oxford: Oxford University Press, 2010.

———. *Jesus in the Talmud.* Princeton: Princeton University Press, 2007.

Schwartz, Joshua. "The Material Realities of Jewish Life in the Land of Israel, c. 235–638." In *The Cambridge History of Judaism,* edited by Steven Katz, vol. 4, 431–56. Cambridge: Cambridge University Press, 2006.

Schwartz, Seth. "Rabbinization in the Sixth Century." In *The Talmud Yerushalmi and Graeco-Roman Culture,* edited by Peter Schäfer, vol. 3, 55–69. Tübingen: Mohr Siebeck, 2002.

Segal, Alan. *Rebecca's Children: Judaism and Christianity in the Roman World.* Cambridge: Harvard University Press, 1986.

Setzer, Claudia. "The Jews in Carthage and Western North Africa, 66–235 CE." In *The Cambridge History of Judaism,* edited by Steven Katz, vol. 4, 68–74. Cambridge: Cambridge University Press, 2006.

Severus of Minorca: Letter on the Conversion of the Jews. Edited and translated by Scott Bradbury. Oxford: Clarendon Press, 1996.

Shaked, Shaul. "Rabbis in Incantation Bowls." In *The Archaeology and Material Culture of the Babylonian Talmud,* edited by Markham Geller, 97–120. Leiden: Brill, 2015.

Shaked, Shaul et al. *Aramaic Bowl Spells: Jewish Babylonian Aramaic.* Vol. 1. Leiden: Brill, 2013.

Shaw, Brent. *Sacred Violence: African Christians and Sectarians Hatred in the Age of Augustine.* Cambridge: Cambridge University Press, 2011.

Simon, Marcel. "Un document du syncrétisme religieux dans l'Afrique romaine." *Comptes rendus des séances de l'Académie des Inscriptions et Belles-Lettres* 122 (1978): 500–25.

———. *Verus Israël: Étude sur les relations entre chrétiens et juifs dans l'Empire Romain (135–425).* Paris: Editions E. De Boccard, 1964 [1948].

Sirat, Colette et al. *La Ketouba de Cologne: Un contrat de mariage juif à Antinoopolis.* Opladen: Westdeutscher, 1986.

Sivan, Hagith. "Between Gaza and Minorca: The (Un) Making of Minorities in Late Antiquity." In *Jews, Christians, and the Roman Empire: The Poetics of Power in Late Antiquity,* edited by Natalie Dohrmann and Annette Yoshiko Reed, 121–36. Philadelphia: University of Pennsylvania Press, 2013.

———. "From Byzantine to Persian Jerusalem: Jewish Perspectives and Jewish/Christian Polemics." *Greek, Roman and Byzantine Studies* 41 (2000): 277–306.

Smelik, William. "The Languages of Roman Palestine." In *The Oxford Handbook of Jewish Daily Life in Roman Palestine,* edited by Catherine Hezser, 122–41. Oxford: Oxford University Press, 2010.

Stemberger, Gunter. "Hieronymus und die Juden seiner Zeit." In *Judaica Minora,* edited by Gunter Stemberger, vol. 2, 347–64. Tübingen: Mohr Siebeck, 1993.

———. *Jews and Christians in the Holy Land: Palestine in the Fourth Century.* Edinburgh: T&T Clark, 1999.

Stern, Menahem. *Greek and Latin Authors on Jews and Judaism.* Jerusalem: Jerusalem Academic Press, 1980.

Stocking, Rachel. "Early Medieval Christian Identity and Anti-Judaism: The Case of the Visigothic Kingdom." *Religion Compass* 2 (2008): 642–58.

Strack, Hermann and Gunter Stemberger. *Introduction to the Talmud and Midrash.* Minneapolis: Fortress Press, 1996.

Stroumsa, Guy. "Jewish Survival in Late Antique Alexandria." In *Jews in Byzantium: Dialects of Minority and Majority Cultures,* edited by Robert Bonfil et al., 257–69. Leiden: Brill, 2012.

Talgam, Rina. *Mosaics of Faith. Floors of Pagans, Jews, Samaritans, Christians, and Muslims in the Holy Land.* Jerusalem: Yad ben Zvi, 2014.

Tcherikover, Victor. Corpus Papyrorum Judaicarum. Vol. 1. Cambridge: Harvard University Press, 1957 (= I CPJ).

Tcherikover, Victor et al. Corpus Papyrorum Judaicarum. Vol. 3. Cambridge: Harvard University Press, 1964 (= III CPJ).

Toch, Michael. *The Economic History of European Jews: Late Antiquity and Early Middle Ages.* Leiden: Brill, 2013.

Tolan, John et al. *Jews in Early Christian Law: Byzantium and the Latin West, 6th–11th Centuries.* Turnhout: Brepols, 2014.

Tromba, Enrico. *La sinagoga dei giudei in epoca romana: Presenza ebraica a Reggio Calabria e provincia.* Reggio Calabria: Istar, 2001.

Van Bekkum, Wout. "The Hebrew Liturgical Poetry of Byzantine Palestine: Recent Research and New Perspectives." *Prooftexts* 28 (2008): 232–46.

Van Haelst, Joseph. *Catalogue des papyrus littéraires juifs et chrétiens.* Paris: Publications de la Sorbonne, 1976.

Vilella, Josep and Pere Barreda. "Los cánones de la Hispana atribuidos a un concilio iliberritano: Estudio filológico." In *I Concili della Cristianità Occidentale: Secoli III-V. XXX Incontro di Studiosi dell'Antichità Cristiana, Roma 3-5 maggio 2001*, 545–79. Rome: Institutum Patristicum Augustinianum, 2002.

Vilozni, Naama. "The Art of the Aramaic Incancation Bowls." In *Aramaic Bowl Spells Jewish Babylonian Aramaic Bowls*, edited by Shaul Shaked, vol. 1, 29–37. Leiden: Brill, 2013.

Werlin, Steven. *Ancient Synagogues of Southern Palestine, 300–800 CE.* Leiden: Brill, 2015.

Yerushalmi, Yosef. *Zakhor. Jewish History and Jewish Memory.* Seattle: Universisty of Washington Press, 1982.

Yuval, Israel. *Two Nations in Your Womb: Perception of Jews and Christians in Late Antiquity and the Middle Ages.* Berkeley: University of California Press, 2006.

Yuval-Hacham, Noa. " 'You shall not make for yourself…': On Jewish Iconoclasm in Late Antiquity." *Ars Judaica* 6 (2010): 7–22.

Zeumer, Karl. *Leges Visigothorum, MGH.* Hannover, 1902.

Zweig, Stefan. *The Buried Candelabrum.* New York: Viking Press, 1937.

Printed and bound by CPI Group (UK) Ltd, Croydon, CR0 4YY

25/03/2025

14647339-0003